SUNSHINE AND SHADOW

MARY PICKFORD *A recent photograph*

Sunshine
and Shadow

BY MARY PICKFORD

Foreword by Cecil B. de Mille

WILLIAM HEINEMANN LTD

LONDON MELBOURNE TORONTO

FIRST PUBLISHED 1956

SET ON THE INTERTYPE FOTOSETTER
PRINTED IN GREAT BRITAIN BY
LOWE AND BRYDONE (PRINTERS) LIMITED,
LONDON, N.W.10

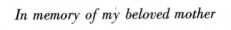

In memory of my beloved mother

FOREWORD
BY CECIL B. DE MILLE

Somewhere, sometime, a phrase was born: "America's sweetheart."

Thousands of such phrases are born daily in Hollywood. Most of them, mercifully, die young.

About once in a generation such a phrase lives, because it is more than a phrase: it is a fact.

I do not know who first called Mary Pickford "America's sweetheart," but, whoever he was, he put in two words the most remarkable personal achievement of its kind in the history of motion pictures.

There have been hundreds of stars. There have been scores of fine actresses in motion pictures. There has been only one Mary Pickford.

To find a comparable name, it is necessary to go from motion pictures to the stage and remember what Maude Adams meant to a whole generation of playgoers. I imagine Mary Pickford would be the first to agree that to compare any name with that of Maude Adams is to put it on a summit where there is room for only one.

What is it that gives a Maude Adams on the stage or a Mary Pickford on the screen the absolutely unique position that no other actress in her time can challenge? Sheer acting ability? No. What they meant to millions is something that goes beyond technique or conscious artistry. In their way they belong in that small but highly potent group of individuals, never more than a handful in any generation, who fire the imagination of millions because, somehow, they respond to something very deep in the minds and hearts of their contemporaries. They become living symbols, charged with power. Such a symbol is "America's sweetheart."

Mary Pickford may smile when she reads this bit of amateur psychology. Yet it is surely the explanation of her enduring hold upon the affections of the American people. She is loved because in her screen career she typified, more than anyone else in motion pictures has ever typified, the kind of person we all want to love.

Those who know Mary Pickford know that her public's image of her is a true one.

When Mary presented me with the Academy Award for *The Greatest Show on Earth* in 1953, she seemed just a little dismayed when I mentioned how long I have known her. Perhaps it was ungallant of me not to explain to the vast television and radio audience that when Mary and I played together in *The Warrens of Virginia* on the New York stage, Mary had the part of my very much younger sister. But Mary should not

10

be worried about anyone's counting years. It will be a good many years before she is as old as I am now; but even then she will still and always be the image of girlhood.

In this book Mary Pickford tells her own story. No doubt it will contain surprises for some who knew Mary only as a figure on the screen, a winsome, expressive face framed in curls. But it will be no surprise to those who know her well to see her revealed also as a very practical person, a good businesswoman, and a good citizen, and also a very thoughtful person, who has pondered the deep things in life and has transmuted her experiences—not all of them happy—into a serene philosophy that serves her well. If Mary Pickford is the eternal image of girlhood, she is also a very real woman.

There is one great trouble with autobiography. No one can tell the whole truth about his own life. I am not thinking about skeletons in closets. I am thinking rather about the things which most of us would find harder to tell than our failings and deficiencies. I mean the good things we have done, if we have done any. If, as Shakespeare says, the good we do is oft interred with our bones, that may be so because sensible people find it as painful and embarrassing to trumpet their good deeds as they would to expose their very bones to public view.

Mary Pickford is a sensible and sensitive person. I daresay she will talk freely about her mistakes. She may make fun of herself on occasion. What she will not tell is the full story of her philanthropies or her patriotic services to her country or all the honors and tributes she has deservedly won, not only from the motion-picture industry, but from the world.

It is a matter of record that Mary Pickford has earned very large sums of money. What the public does not know, and will not learn from her, is the large amount of it which she has given away to charities.

Many of her fans have seen her, glamorous, appealing, convincing, on platforms in their towns and cities, taking part in government-bond drives and other patriotic activities. What they may not stop to realize, and what they will never learn from her lips or pen, is what one of those bond tours costs in terms of the sheer wear and tear of having to be glamorous and appealing and convincing three or four times a day in different places for weeks on end.

Among my own memories of Mary Pickford I cherish particularly one that she has probably completely forgotten. One evening in 1945 I was asked to speak at the Biltmore Hotel in Los Angeles about why I had chosen to sacrifice my right to work in radio rather than pay a $1.00 political assessment to my union. My stand on that question was, to say the least, not enthusiastically supported by all my fellow-workers in the motion-picture and radio industries. On the evening in question the meeting hall was packed to the doors; and it was packed in another sense, also, by some strategically placed hecklers. I saw a woman struggling to get through the crowd, patiently but indomitably working her way, squeezing between chairs and packed bodies, not being stopped by anything. It was Mary Pickford, come to take her place on the platform beside me. I had not asked her to come. I did not know she was coming. But she had heard about the meeting and, unlike many others, Mary did not pause to calculate whether the gesture would be popular or unpopular. It was a chance to stand up and be counted for political freedom and the right to work. And she was there.

Show business has a term to describe someone like Mary Pickford. She is a good trouper. As often happens, show business hides its heart under a glib phrase. There is another word for being a good trouper, a word that show business would think too grand to use. That word is dedication.

And that word, I think, is Mary Pickford's secret, as it is the secret of anyone who succeeds at anything. Most of us serve our ideals by fits and starts. The person who makes a success of living is the one who sees his goal steadily and aims for it unswervingly. That is dedication. Mary Pickford's story shows what it has meant in her life.

When Mary's publisher asked me to write this foreword, I replied that Mary is one person of whom it can be most truly said that she needs no introduction! If any readers bear with me this far, they will by now be in the same impatient state as a motion picture audience waiting for "our Mary" to appear on the screen. It is time for the unnecessary introducer to step aside, not satisfied that he has done justice to his subject, but grateful for the opportunity of paying his tribute to America's sweetheart and to a friendship that goes back to her childhood.

Your patience will be rewarded. Here she is.

ILLUSTRATIONS

17

19

20

SUNSHINE AND SHADOW

PROLOGUE TO A FAMILY

To the best of my knowledge only two persons
have answered from earliest infancy to the name
of Mary Pickford. One was a great aunt of mine who was killed
by a tram in London at the age of seven. The other was a little
Eskimo boy who was evidently given the name in a confusion
resulting from the male role I played in *Little Lord Fauntleroy*.
The story was told me by a friend of mine who had traveled
extensively in the Far North. One day as he was passing an
Eskimo hut a boy of three, giggling merrily and naked as the
day he was born, dashed through an open doorway into the
lane outside. An anxious mother followed in hot pursuit. My
friend watched in amusement till he heard the Eskimo mother
scream out a name. In utter disbelief he listened again, and
once more the name rang out in the crisp morning air, "Mary
Pickford!"

As it happens, that little rebellious son of the North had
more right to the name than I. For I did not take the name of

Mary Pickford till I was thirteen years old, and then only at the insistence of David Belasco, who cordially disapproved of my real name. I suppose I have no cause to regret Mr. Belasco's judgment. My real name was Gladys Smith.

I asked Mother one day how I happened to be called "Gladys" instead of plain "Anne" or "Jane" or "Mary" Smith. "Your aunt Lizzie," said Mother, "was reading a popular novel just before you were born, and the heroine was a Scotch girl named Lady Gladys."

I took the name by which I have long been known to the public from my Irish grandfather, John Pickford Hennessey, who came of a comparatively rich family from Tralee, County Kerry, in the south of Ireland. My grandmother was also born in Tralee, but she was a miller's daughter and very poor. Had the two of them remained in Ireland they would never have met; they moved in entirely different social worlds. They met in Quebec, Canada, fell instantly in love, and were married.

When my great-grandmother Hennessey received the news of their marriage, she disowned her son and vowed never to speak to him again. This vow she kept till the day she died. It was she who bequeathed the name of "Pickford" to my grandfather.

Grandma Hennessey was Catherine Faeley before she married Grandpa Hennessey. In Tralee she had lived the simple, humble life of an Irish village girl of a century ago. Then, every Irish family of the small towns had its story teller and Grandma Hennessey was the pride of the Faeleys in the vaunted Irish art of twisting a commonplace into a humorous tale. She had a fabulous memory and was a sidesplitting mimic. These talents she passed on to Mother, who possessed a remarkable gift for dramatizing a triviality and finding a suitable saying for every situation. I shall never forget one expression that remained in the family like a cherished heirloom: "I won't stop now till I make a show of meself with clothes." I believe the story behind that saying is worth retelling.

The time of one of the great droughts had come, and the Faeleys decided to send their daughter Catherine to Canada, taking advantage of the free passage provided by the English Government.

Grandma Hennessey had never owned a new dress in her whole life, only the perennial hand-me-downs of the family, and there she was being bundled off to Canada, with hardly a presentable stitch to her back. So my great-grandmother Faeley went on a spending binge one day and paid an itinerant peddler fifty cents a piece for two lengths of cotton. Then she sat herself down and made Catherine two dresses. The moment one of them was finished Catherine slipped into it and went cavorting up and down in the back of the house, at the same time watching her shadow on the wall. A little girl next door studied her for a few moments and then shouted out to her:

"Catherine, what are you doing there?"

"Oh, faith," says Catherine, "it's one of me two new dresses. Sure, and I'm not going to shtop now till I make a show of meself with clothes."

That's been proverbial in our family ever since. If anyone of us ever was extravagant or indulged in any needless luxury, the others would shake their heads solemnly and say, "Sure, that one won't stop now until she makes a show of herself with clothes."

It was my Irish grandmother Hennessey, little Catherine

25

Faeley, who was the warrior in the family; my mother inherited her positive nature, and I suppose I did too. She was a devout Catholic who lived her faith in her heart and practiced it in good deeds. Mother told me in later years how Grandma Hennessey would go into brothels to persuade the girls to go back to their mothers. She would actually go without the bare necessities to provide those unfortunates with whatever they needed for their journey home.

"Does your mother know about this thing?" she would ask them.

"No, and that's why I can never go home."

And Grandma would say, "Well, the past is the past; close the book, make up your mind to talk to no one about it. Go home to your mother and begin life all over again."

The girls often wept and said they were too ashamed to face their parents and friends again.

"Be ashamed!" Grandma Hennessey would say. "Cleanse yourself in every way and walk with your head high towards the new life that awaits you. God is on the side of every penitent sinner."

That was Grandma's contribution to God. She would even take them to church with her and have the priest talk to them. If there were children, and the mothers were Catholic, she would have them baptized.

As for the English side of my family, my father (one of twelve children) used to say that if he ever were arrested he would probably be fined for contempt of court when he gave his name as "John Smith."

Grandmother Smith arrived in Canada when she was six years of age. For the next eighty years of her life she attended the same Methodist church with the strictest regularity, stopping at the age of eighty-six to spend the remaining five years of her life meditating at home. Her husband, Joseph Smith, came from Liverpool. The Smiths were people of considerable wealth and they sailed from England and up the St. Lawrence in their own sailing vessel when Grandpa Smith was a baby.

I would fly as though a demon were after me when I heard Grandma Smith rustling through the house. I remember her always in a black silk dress and purple taffeta petticoat—the violets on her wee bonnet matching the underskirt. It seems to me she was never without her black kid gloves and a small beaded silk bag.

Grandma Smith looked very much like Queen Victoria—same height, same imperial girth, and she was just as formidable and strait-laced. One of her horrors was to see people enjoying themselves on the Sabbath. There was really very little a family like ours *could* do on Sunday. Taking the belt-line trolley that encircled Toronto was about the only amusement. But that was enough for Grandma. For years she served on a citizens' committee to urge passage of a law against the operation of street cars on the Sabbath.

Between these two stalwart grandmothers—one Catholic and the other Protestant—I came very near to going unbaptized. My first baptism took place, actually, because a kind priest named Father Murphy knocked on the door one day when I was seriously ill.

"Sorry, Father, but you cannot come in," said Mother. "We're quarantined. Black diphtheria."

"Who is it?"

"My little girl Gladys."

"I'm not afraid of the contagion," said Father Murphy, "but if I came in it would be unfair to others I might contact later. How old is your daughter?"

"Just four, Father."

"Of course she's baptized, Mrs. Smith?"

"No, Father," said Mother, embarrassed. "You see, my husband is Protestant and——"

"Four years old, in danger of death, and not baptized! I'm coming in!"

Father Murphy entered into my bedroom, put his cool hand on my brow and to the very outspoken delight of Grandma Hennessey I was baptized Gladys Marie Smith. I remember turning on my right side and falling instantly asleep. When I awakened a great peace had come over me. I was healed.

Mother had been greatly worried about my not being baptized, but the decision had been Father Murphy's, and she never told my father. After Father died, Mother did something that was so typical of her fair-mindedness. She had all three of us baptized in the Protestant faith, as a tribute to the memory of my father.

I was always old beyond my years. One night, when I was only three, my aunt Lizzie found me on the street corner in my nightgown, dangling my feet over the edge of the curb.

"Precious," she said to me, "what in the world are you doing out here at this hour of the night?"

"I'm 'frinking,' Auntie," I said.

"Do your mama and papa know you're here?"

My birthplace in Toronto

And I replied, "Oh no!"

She put an arm around me and said, "You've got to go right back to bed now."

I shook my head. "No, Auntie, I've got to stay here and 'frink.'"

It seemed to me that if I thought hard enough and long enough I'd remember where I came from. "Wherever it is I came from," I remember saying to myself, "it must be lots and lots better than here, and I want to go back but where do I begin?"

I must have been very young indeed when I began to "frink" about God. I also thought a good deal about the devil, who as far as I could learn was waiting around the corner just to snatch my soul. I was then attending my English grandmother's Methodist church and it seemed to me the time had come to settle this God and devil business. One bright Sunday morning, in my freshly starched undies and squeaky boots, my sister Chuckie's hand firmly in mine, I marched on the Sunday school and flung a challenge at the teacher:

"Which is stronger," I demanded to know, "God or the devil?"

Her face frozen with shock, my teacher replied, "Why, God, of course. He is all-powerful."

"Well," I said, undismayed, "why doesn't He kill the devil so I wouldn't be a bad little girl any more and have to go to the hot place?"

I know positively that I would not have been in the theater if father had lived. For one thing, we would probably all have remained in Toronto. Father was a very charming man, handsome, gay, lovable, with curly golden-brown hair, and graceful, delicate hands that must have been destined for better things. While I was still suffering from my siege of black diphtheria, it seems there was a terrible depression in Canada. As I look back now, there was nothing but depressions—for the Smith clan at any rate.

To make some extra money, Father worked all night in a local theater, pulling up scenery until he got big blisters on those graceful hands of his. Mother told me this later; I don't remember it myself. But I do remember the first money he gave me: he was standing beside me telling me to open my hands, and into them he put the seventy-five cents he had earned that night. Seventy-five cents then was probably worth more than five dollars today. Of course I gave it to Mother, but with a sense of great pride. Another recollection of the early lure of money was the time my sister Lottie dropped a Canadian five-cent silver piece between the keys of Mother's beloved upright piano. The thought of this buried treasure tormented me so that I was determined to break all the keys to retrieve the priceless coin. Grandma caught me going from the kitchen to the "parlor," a look of high resolve on my face and a hammer in my hand.

Whenever I got a penny, at the age of five or six, I would go to the florist and buy myself a rosebud, which I took home and carefully tended. One day, after making my purchase, I pointed to a full-blown rose that seemed to be falling, and asked the florist, "May I have that rose, if you don't want it any more?" The florist gave it to me, for nothing, and that became quite a ritual: my rosebud for a penny, and a fading rose for the asking. After repeating this performance three or four

Mother

Father

times the florist asked me one day what I did with the rose that he no longer wanted.

"I eat it," I told him.

And that was the simple truth. It had tasted very bitter at first, but I thought that if I were to eat it, the beauty and the color and the perfume would somehow get inside me.

This intense response to beautiful colors and shapes once made me steal. It was a goldfish, and I was six years old. I had been sent to the store for birdseed for our bird Enza ("I opened the cage and influenza"). There I saw this flashing bit of sunlight—a very small fish, glistening in its fierce beauty. I grabbed it with my hot, grubby hand and flew as on the wings of a fallen angel.

It was a long way home, over a mile, and uphill. I opened the front door, raced upstairs, and of course the only place that I could find water, and that quickly, was the toilet. Lovingly and carefully I placed my goldfish in its new aquarium. But the little fish I gazed down at with such panting expectations was no longer his own flashing, wriggling beautiful self. There he floated, and Grandma Hennessey, who wondered what all the commotion was about, looked over my shoulder and broke the news to me that he was dead.

Mother had always boasted that the Smith children wouldn't steal a pin. It wasn't until I was well along in my twenties that I dared confess to her that I once stole a goldfish.

My conscience also hurts me for a spanking I once deserved but my sister received. In the parlor, on an easel, was a monstrous sketch of my father. Over the top of the picture Mother had lovingly draped a yellow silk scarf with yellow floss tassels. One afternoon, having nothing better to do, I moistened my fingers with my tongue, stood on my tiptoes, and very meticulously rolled the tassels between my forefinger and thumb—the brilliant idea being to make them look like golden ringlets. Much to my disappointment the result of my afternoon's labor was a scraggly assortment of dirty little wads.

Mother was horrified when she discovered that little bit of vandalism. Without asking who was the culprit she snatched my sister up and gave her a thorough warming. I can still see my sister's face—a picture of outraged innocence. I finally stuttered out the truth. But Mother's wrath had already been vented. Very quietly she took me on her lap and gave me a long lecture, but she didn't spank me, though I certainly deserved it, for not coming forward in time to prevent the wrong

34

that was done Lottie. Perhaps I was spared any physical discipline because I had been so desperately ill. The truth is, I don't remember that Mother ever spanked me. A rebuke from her was much worse punishment than any she could have administered with her hands.

That tampering with the yellow floss tassels of Mother's silk scarf may have been the inspiration for what later became the Pickford curls—and poor Lottie had to pay the piper.

1

Mother was still in her middle twenties when she became a widow with three baby children and Grandma Hennessey, an invalid, to support. My father worked as purser on the steamship line that runs from Toronto to Lewiston near Niagara Falls. One day he bounded down the stairs to the deck below, not noticing a pulley dangling overhead. It struck him a fearful blow, causing a blood clot on his brain. Small as our resources were, Mother sent to what we called "the States" for the best doctors. They tried everything they knew at that time to dissolve the clot, but without success.

I can close my eyes now and hear that scream of Mother's at the moment my father passed on. And I can still see myself climbing out of bed and going down the hall and looking in the door. I was the first to arrive on the scene, and I shall never forget the sickening sense of horror that swept through me. There was Mother shrieking hysterically and beating her head against the wall. She had long, thick, silken hair that fell down past her waist. It was streaming over her face, which had been cut apparently as she hit her head against the wall in her grief; her dressing gown was covered with blood. Through the streaming hair I could see the wild look on Mother's face. But in all her sobbing she never noticed that I was standing in the doorway. I had not the slightest suspicion of what had happened. I gazed at my father lying in his bed and I thought he was sleeping. Finally Mother's sister Lizzie heard the pounding and screaming, dashed up the stairs from the floor below, glanced into the bedroom and was startled to find me standing there, petrified with fear. Snatching me up hurriedly, she took me back into her bedroom and rocked me to sleep in her arms. The rest of the family went to Mother's rescue.

The next thing I knew it was early morning. As Aunt Lizzie carried me down to breakfast, she turned my head away from Father's bedroom. And at that moment somehow I knew what had happened. I refused to eat my breakfast, jumped down from my chair and, crying hysterically for "my papa," wedged myself between the serving table and the wall of the dining room. Most dreadful of all was the day they lifted me up to kiss my father good-by. What a barbarous practice to inflict on children! Yet, as I looked, I remember telling myself that I must photograph his features on my mind. Father had been such a handsome man and Mother adored him.

One of my most vivid childhood memories is of my mother and father going out one night to dinner or to a ball. It was a rare adventure for them. I recall how pretty my mother was

Me, Mabel Watson, Mother, Lottie, Edith Watson, Jack

in a pink silk dress she had made herself—her beautiful blue-black hair piled high on top of her head. Father wore a dinner jacket. And I remember how handsome he was.

In those days it was my father I loved. I didn't really care so much about my mother. She was always too busy to play with me. There were three babies under the age of four, myself, my younger sister Lottie, and the baby, Jack. Grandma Hennessey also lived with us was mending and sewing and cooking and washing—a wearisome all-day routine that started over and over again but never ended. Children don't take that into account when they feel somehow neglected by their mothers. But Father could find time for us.

And then I was luckier than my sister and brother, because I was wanted from the moment they knew I was on the way. My poor little sister Lottie, nicknamed Chuckie, came fourteen months later, when money was still scarcer in the family and my mother had hoped for a boy. I've been told how Father came home the day Lottie was born and asked Mother where the new baby was.

"Oh," said Mother wearily, "I suppose she's in her crib."

In those days childbirth was not easy. Lottie weighed ten pounds.

My father, studying Mother's face, asked, "What's the matter? Is there anything wrong with the baby?"

And Mother replied, "Oh no; it's just another girl, that's all."

Father picked up the small bundle, his eyes smiling down at it.

"Why, she's a beautiful baby! You ought to be ashamed of yourself, Lottie." Then he turned his gaze back to my sister

At fourteen months

and said, "Never mind, darling, you'll always be your papa's own little baby. My little 'Chuckie.'"

And she was always just that. This was my first experience with jealousy—my first sting of the serpent. Father never let little Lottie forget that she was "Papa's own little baby. My Chuckie baby." I remember how he used to get off the streetcar in the evening and Chuckie would run like mad to him and he would scoop her up in his arms. I would walk up to him sedately, or even stand still and wait for him to approach me. I suppose I was a mean little girl doing that, but I knew deep down in my four-year-old heart that I played second fiddle to my sister, and that made me miserable. But it was right and just that it should be so. As I was the delicate one, everybody else spoiled and pampered me, especially my aunt Lizzie and Grandma Hennessey.

When Father died I realized, with a strange and frightening suddenness, that Mother was alone, and I decided that I had to do something about it. "I should be helping Mother," I remember telling myself one day. I put down a doll I was playing with and went into the large kitchen-living room.

"Mama," I said, "have you next month's rent, and money for the coal?"

Mother was bent over the sewing machine hurrying to finish a dress. Since Father's death she had taken up dress making and was now busier than ever, scraping together a meagre livelihood. Abstractly she answered, "No, darling, but don't worry, we'll get somehow." I don't believe she even realized she was speaking to me.

Mother went on with her sewing, but I withdrew into my shell. In those days I would hide away from the rest of the family, wrapping myself in the red chenille drapes in the hall. Aunt Lizzie found me a few hours later curled up in the drapes, crying my heart out.

"What in the world is wrong, precious?"

"Mama doesn't have enough money for the rent," I sobbed.

Aunt Lizzie shook her head angrily and stormed into the kitchen.

"Lottie," she said, "you've just got to stop letting that child hear those things!"

42

"What things?" said Mother without raising her head from the sewing machine.

"That you don't have money for food or rent. . . ."

"Oh, Lizzie, I didn't mean to say it; I was so busy and distracted. How dreadful!"

"She's getting thinner and paler every day," said Aunt Lizzie, "and worrying about money isn't going to help her get any better."

Mother was never caught off her guard again. After that, whenever I asked her about the rent, and about money for coal and food, she would give me a reassuring smile and say, "Oh yes, darling, I have plenty of money. Don't you worry. Now go out and play with the other children."

During many of my illnesses we had Dr. G. B. Smith, who was head of the Children's Hospital of Toronto. I believe Mother later estimated that this man, who was known as "Little G. B.," had saved my life four times. I remember I wasn't yet seven when I became terribly anemic after one of my attacks. I would lie down on the floor and go to sleep wherever I happened to be. When Mother noticed I was having night-sweats she took me to the clinic. God bless those clinics! I've always been so appreciative of the privilege of going there—because it was there they discovered I had a spot on my lung. They told Mother that if she had let it go a little longer, it might have been too late. Medicine was prescribed, and Mother saw to it that I also got the special food that Dr. Smith recommended. It wasn't long before I had fully recovered.

One day Dr. Smith came to see Mother. He began by reminding her that he and his wife were childless; that for some

*The cameraman thought me idiotic enough to believe
there was "a little birdie in the black box"—
hence the furious expression.*

time now they had been thinking the matter over and had finally come to a decision. Would Mother consent to their adopting me? They would give me every advantage beyond Mother's reach, and since their name was Smith too there wouldn't be any need of changing mine. Mother politely but firmly and promptly refused.

"I couldn't think of it, Dr. Smith," she said.

Later, she reported the whole thing to Aunt Lizzie, who lashed out at her:

"You have no right to stand in her way. All my life I have regretted that our mother and father didn't allow me to go to that rich couple who wanted to adopt me."

So Mother dressed me up in my best bib and tucker and took me to Dr. Smith's house. On the streetcar and during the short walk to the doctor's house I noticed that Mother, usually very talkative, was pale and silent. The house was large, comfortable, and extremely well furnished. I was shown the pretty little bedroom that was to become mine.

"You can have anything you want, Gladys," said Dr. and Mrs. Smith.

"A pony and cart?"

"Yes."

"Chicken every day?"

They assured me I could, and ice cream too.

Mother said nothing throughout the interview. While waiting for the streetcar I said gleefully to Mother, "Think how Chuckie and Johnny will love that pony and cart! And you and Grandma can have half of my chicken, and we'll all be rich and happy."

"No, darling," said Mother. "We won't be there. You see,

you'll be Dr. Smith's little girl, and Chuckie and Jack will stay with Mother."

Mother was kneeling down in the grass in front of me to look me straight in the eyes. The sidewalk was lined with shady trees, beautiful big chestnut trees, and she went on explaining how I wouldn't be her little girl any more, but Dr. Smith's. . . . I felt a terror clutching at my heart.

"Mama," I said, "don't you want me any more?"

With that she started to cry.

"I'll always want you, darling, but I can't give you the pony and cart, and I can't give you chicken and ice cream every day. . . ."

I stopped her. "I don't want to be Dr. Smith's little girl and I don't like ponies and I want to go home with you, Mama!"

And Mother took out a handkerchief and wiped away my tears and hers, and with a very determined set of her shoulders she said:

"That's the end of that, and I'm certainly going to tell your aunt Lizzie a thing or two. There will be no more of this nonsense."

If you only knew how my mother loved me. You see, as a baby, I looked like my daddy. In later years she told me that when the pain of losing my father was too great for her, she would put me on the table and study my face, my features being so much like his.

A determination was born in me the day of our visit to Dr. Smith that nothing could crush: I must try to take my father's place in some mysterious way, and prevent anything from breaking up my family. There then began a devotion for my mother that the passing years only made stronger and deeper.

In years to come we were to be known as the Four Musketeers
—Mother, my sister Lottie, my brother Jack, and myself. When
the money began to come in, we had one pocketbook for it,
and Mother remained the custodian to the end.

I never had any young companions my age except for my
brother and sister. Also as Mother and I grew closer Lottie
and Johnny banded together against us. All this matured me
very early, I suppose, but it cheated me of any real childhood.

I am grateful this was not so with my brother and sister,
and I have treasured a remark Jack made to me one morning
in my dressing room during the filming of *Little Lord Fauntleroy*. He was sitting beside me as I was brushing my curls before going on the movie set. I noticed that he was studying me
intently in the mirror. Our eyes finally met and he said:

"You poor kid, you've never lived, have you?"

"Certainly I have," I said. "I'm doing exactly what I always
wanted to do."

"Well, I don't know. You see, if Chuckie and I were bumped
off tomorrow, the world would owe us nothing. We've had a
million laughs. You've had everything, yes, but, Mary, you've
never really lived. And you don't know how to play."

I don't believe I was more than five years old when I became Mother's deputy, a kind of little mother.

Bringing up Johnny and Chuckie was a very serious business to me. The thought of the two of them playing in the street
with dirty hands and faces would distress me. I can't recall the
number of times I chased them back into the house to tidy
them up.

47

2

It wasn't long after Father's death that Mother decided to rent the master bedroom, as there was plenty of space in that large house for the family.

One day a well-dressed man applied for the vacant room. Up to then the room had been occupied only by women. But this man explained that he was married and he was sure Mother would like his wife. The pros and cons of the situation were warmly debated by Mother, Aunt Lizzie, and Grandma. They finally agreed that renting the room under these circumstances would be quite respectable—a decision which was probably the greatest turning point in my life. The man in question was the stage manager of the Cummings Stock Company of Toronto.

One day, about two weeks after the couple were installed, the man asked Mother if he could have a moment with her.

"Mrs. Smith," he began, "you may have read in the papers that I'm producing a play called *The Silver King.*"

"I believe I have."

"Well, would you consider letting your two little girls appear in a schoolroom scene?"

Mother was highly indignant.

"I'm sorry," she said, "but I will never allow my innocent babies to associate with actresses who smoke."

"I respect your misgivings, Mrs. Smith," the man said, "but will you do me a favor before you make a final decision?"

"It's completely out of the question. The thought of those infants making a spectacle of themselves on a public stage! . . ."

"This is all I ask, Mrs. Smith. Come backstage with us tonight. I assure you that professional people are no different from any others. They are good, bad, and indifferent like the rest of the world. This happens to be a very happy and respectable group of actors and actresses who have been together a long time."

Mother made the daring trip backstage that night and was evidently impressed by the behavior of the people in the company. The result of that tour of inspection was that Lottie and I made our debut in the theater in a play called *The Silver King*.

I played two parts. In the first act I was a villainous little girl who was mean to Cissy Denver, the Silver King's daughter. My opening line on stage was:

"Don't speak to her, girls; her father killed a man!"—a statement accompanied by a smart stamp of the foot, in which I had been very meticulously coached. My sister Lottie's function in the play was just as elaborate, but without words. Hers

As Cissy Denver in "The Silver King"

50

was the kindly gesture of handing Cissy a stick of peppermint candy and giving her a pat on the back.

In the last act I played Cissy's brother, Ned Denver, a part without lines in which I was supposed to sit very quietly on stage while my father, the "Silver King," had a secret conversation with his wife. I had been carefully instructed to play with a set of wooden blocks and a toy horse and make myself as inconspicuous as possible. Instead I built the blocks into a giant pyramid and ran the toy horse into them. The "Denvers" were startled by my sudden improvisation, and the audience must have laughed more at the expressions on their faces than at me.

When the final curtain fell, the stage manager came up to me and said, "You were a very smart little girl to think of that piece of business."

"Thank you, sir," I said.

"You got yourself the biggest laugh of the evening."

"Thank you, sir," I repeated, beginning to feel that I was a very great actress indeed.

"Yes, you were very clever tonight," he went on, pitching his voice to a grave tone, "but don't ever steal a scene from a fellow actor again."

"Oh, I would never do that, sir!"

"Do you realize you spoiled the speeches of the Silver King and his wife?"

"No, sir."

". . . that the audience didn't hear what they had to say? That so long as you stay in the theater you must never draw attention away from the main action?"

"Yes, sir," I said, feeling very deflated.

"But I'm going to do something irregular, Gladys," said the stage manager. "I'm going to let you keep that little piece of 'business' in."

And he told me the spot where I could get my laugh without interfering with the other players.

That was my first lecture in the good manners and ethics of the theater. I was only five years old, but the lesson sank in and I don't think I ever forgot it. To this day I don't like a scene stealer, even when it is myself.

The first Christmas after Father died Lottie and I were confident Santa Claus would visit us as usual. Since we had, in our own opinion, been very, very good girls, we requested and expected to get two identical doll carriages and two lovely sleeping dolls. Jack wanted a dancing bear. Christmas morning was cold, dark, and snowy. It was about six o'clock when the three of us tumbled out of bed. I remember smelling the rare and delicious perfume of oranges as we ran downstairs to the warm kitchen where Mother and Grandma Hennessey were waiting for us. Mother, I found out later, had not been to bed at all that night, and neither had Grandma.

There were the two carriages, the sleeping dolls, and the dancing bear. We also found oranges and raisins and little hard candies; a whistle, a rubber ball, and right on top of each stocking a candy man.

I was a good deal older before I learned how Mother with her dressmaker's pittance had managed such a miracle.

Four weeks before Christmas, with no money to buy any of the presents we wanted, Mother displayed her usual courage and initiative. Spying a doll carriage in a nearby shop, she walked in and offered the manager a large, standing screen embroidered with chrysanthemums (I believe she also offered to embroider a stork) in exchange for two carriages.

The screen, of course, had to be made after a hard day's work housekeeping and dressmaking. (How many midnight hours must have gone into that embroidery and what I wouldn't give to possess that screen today!)

When Christmas Eve arrived Mother owned the doll carriages—but nothing else. There were no dolls and no money —not even for a meager Christmas dinner. In despair she and Grandma Hennessey sat in the kitchen, Grandma telling her beads and praying to the Almighty for His beneficent help. Grandma's prayers were answered, for the doorbell rang. Two members of my father's lodge, the Knights of Pythias, greeted Mother on the doorstep and offered $10—her share of a $40 treasury surplus they had decided to divide among the widows of their deceased brothers.

I wonder whether any ten dollars was ever more welcome! Mother flew to the grocery and butcher to get our holiday dinner. Around the corner she found a toy shop still open. Jack got his dancing bear and Lottie and I our dolls in beautiful dresses Mother sewed for them during the night.

I wish those men at the lodge could have known the joy and faith they brought to our family of five that Christmas. It was a beautiful investment which memory has left intact for a lifetime.

Shortly after the Cummings Stock Company moved on to fresh pastures, I was given a role in a variety show—a small, silent, and sleeping role in a one-act play entitled, *The Littlest Girl.*

"The Littlest Girl"

My performance consisted of being carried on the stage and passed from the arms of one actor into the lap of another.

On the same variety bill was a young girl named Elsie Janis. Mother whispered to me in awe that they were paying this girl the unbelievable salary of seventy-five dollars a week. My own salary was fifteen dollars a week. Elsie's repertory included a magnificent imitation of Edna May and another of Anna Held, in brilliant diamonds, knee-length dress, and a white, diamond-studded staff. Mother and I were simply dazzled as Elsie sang, " 'Oh, I just can't make my eyes behave!' " Mother, not wanting to miss so rare an opportunity, took my hand and went in to consult Elsie's Mother as to how one went about preparing for so brilliant a career as her daughter's.

"Take her to see the finest plays and artists," said Mrs. Janis. "But she must never imitate anyone, other than to be a mimic. In anything else, first and above all, let her be herself." That advice served me well in the years that followed. Elsie and I later became and remained good friends and so did our mothers.

Mother, needless to say, had become quite stage-minded by now, and when she read that a new group, the Valentine Stock Company, was going to put on *The Silver King*, she finished her day's work and put me into my Sunday best.

"We're going down to see whether they'll take you for the same parts again, darling."

I had thoughts of my own at that moment, but I said nothing. While we were being interviewed by Miss Anne Blanke, head of the company, much to Mother's mortification, I suddenly spoke up and said:

"I want to play Cissy Denver."

56

To Mother's astonishment Miss Blanke said: "I don't see any reason why you shouldn't."

"But Miss Blanke," interrupted Mother. "She can't read, and it's a long part."

Recognizing a friend and kindred soul, I went over to Miss Blanke and I put my hand in hers and looked up into her face:

"Please, lady, let me try."

This melted my mother.

"Well," she said, "there can't be any harm in trying. We'll begin working on it tonight, but I know she can't remember such a long role."

I had made up my mind that I could and would, and I just had to prove it to Mother. The moment we left the theater and were outside under the lamppost waiting for the streetcar, we set to work. Mother read the lines and cues to me and I repeated them. We were still studying when the streetcar arrived and we continued all the way home. Before I went to bed that night I knew the entire first act by heart.

There was another reason I was so determined to play the role of Cissy Denver. Before our interview with Miss Blanke I had been taken to the matinees of the Valentine Stock Company. I was so little I would sit on my mother's, my Aunt Lizzie's, or my cousin's lap, which enabled me to look over the heads of people in front and saved the price of an extra seat. *The Silver King* was going to be played by a very attractive man named Jack Webster, and the truth of the matter is that I had fallen in love with him. That was all in the back of my mind when I asked for the part of Cissy Denver—Webster was to be my father in the play.

One morning at breakfast Aunt Lizzie looked up from the local newspaper and said, "Oh, poor Jack Webster!"

"What in heaven's name has happened to him?" asked Mother.

"Why, the poor man's been stricken with pneumonia," said my aunt.

At that precise moment my sister Chuckie reached over and took my egg spoon. With that I let forth a howl that would have done a banshee credit, jumped from the table, and flung myself, sobbing, on the couch. The family promptly turned on poor Chuckie and were berating her sharply when my cousin, Mamie, blandly announced:

"She's not crying about the egg spoon. She's crying about Jack Webster being ill."

A few days later I began to cough and to run a high temperature, and sure enough when the doctor was brought in to see me he pronounced it a serious case of pneumonia. I was beside myself with joy. I had absolutely no idea what pneumonia was; I knew only I had the same thing my beloved Jack Webster had. While I was convalescing Miss Blanke offered me a role in *Uncle Tom's Cabin,* and then to my great delight sent a cab to our door to take Mother and me to the theater, my first taste of luxury. I was still quite weak from the pneumonia and they bundled me up in blankets. When we arrived, Jack Webster came out, picked me up, blankets and all, and carried me onto the rehearsal stage. That was perhaps the most triumphal entry of my life. I was so very little at six that I don't think I was as tall as the average child of three. Mr.

As Little Eva in "Uncle Tom's Cabin"

Webster was sweet and gentle with me. As he picked me up he said:

"I'm so glad to see my little baby girl again."

And all I could think of saying in reply was:

"Mr. Webster, I had the very same thing you had."

"Poor little baby," he said, "I know just how you felt."

I never saw Jack Webster after that. I could have seen him in later years, but I wanted to treasure the memory of my first love as I had known it then.

It was while I was playing in *Uncle Tom's Cabin* that my austere grandmother Smith decided to attend the theater. I never learned what she thought of my performance, but to my knowledge this was the first and last time she ever set foot in a theater, until I made a motion picture called *In the Bishop's Carriage*. Grandma thought from the title that it was a religious film. To her horror she discovered that I played the part of a thief. I was told that she almost had a fainting spell when I came out in a short ballet costume. She left the theater hurriedly, and doubtless covered her face in her hasty retreat.

While I adored my Irish grandmother, I must confess that she did not think any better of the theater than Grandma Smith.

If I inherited a love of the stage, it must have been from my Irish grandfather. Mother often told me how long before I was born this jovial Hennessey would stand outside the theater waiting to be the first to enter. One night he persuaded Grandma Hennessey to go along with him. They were seated when a fire wagon went clanging past. Convinced that her house was on fire and that her children were already being consumed by the flames, Grandma rushed from the theater, and with a very irate Grandpa Hennessey in her wake hurried home to find house and family completely unscathed. That was enough theater for Grandma.

"Never again," she announced, "will I pay good money to make a fool of myself watching other people making fools of themselves."

After I started acting I had very little chance for formal schooling. My only real schooling, in fact, took place one winter when I was six at the Louisa Street School in Toronto, which my father and all his brothers and sisters had attended.

In those days Mother often had to leave so early for work that Lottie and I had to wash and dress ourselves. We were always rushed off like mad for school, and we were very often late. I'll never forget the terror of hearing that school bell ring while Lottie and I were still a half block away from our goal. Miss Adams, the principal, had repeatedly conveyed to us how she abhorred tardy pupils. One day when Lottie and I were late twice in succession Miss Adams scolded us viciously and hurled these terrifying words at us:

"The next time you are late, the devil will send a big black wagon for both of you, and you will never see your mother again."

Lottie and I didn't wait to hear another word. We didn't even put on our hats and coats and leggings. With one impulse we dashed out into the subzero weather. Falling and sliding and weeping till the tears froze on our faces, we made for home. Mother, who happened to be home early that morning, was unpacking some purchases in the kitchen, when we came crashing in, leaving the outside door wide open, speechless with terror. Panting and trembling, we finally managed to report what

Miss Adams had said. Mother was quietly furious. Assuring us it was all nonsense, she put warm clothes on Lottie and me and took us back to the schoolroom. When she confronted Miss Adams, she calmly asked whether she had made that monstrous threat about the devil coming to take us off in a big black wagon.

"Most certainly I did, Mrs. Smith," retorted the principal. "And that was very mild to what they deserved."

"And what, in your estimation, Miss Adams, did they deserve?" asked Mother.

"A good, sound thrashing!"

To which Mother very gravely replied that if Miss Adams ever laid a hand on Lottie and me she would not be answerable for what she might do to her; that she was going to the Board of Education the very next day to lodge a complaint against her.

For weeks after that I would jump out of bed at night, screaming, "The black wagon! No, no!"

When, along with those nightmares, my appetite began to fail, Mother thought it time to take me to the doctor, who suggested that I be taken out of school at once. Actually I was so frequently sick and nervous during those years that I was physically unfit to attend school. When the Smith clan embarked on its endless odyssey of the road, all hope of further schooling was abandoned. Mother, who had been carefully taught by the nuns, purchased textbooks and began to instruct me herself. Much of my early facility in reading was acquired from a study of the advertising signs on trains, and I would be unable to estimate the amount of hotel stationery I used to perfect my handwriting. I copied anything I saw that I liked.

This probably helped develop the retentive memory that has been both my blessing and my curse.

Mother was always trying to train my memory too. I remember she used to send me to the corner grocer's and instruct me to make a mental note of everything I saw. I'd come back and try to give a detailed report. My great triumph came the day Mother sent me to Eaton's Department Store in Toronto to buy a spool of pink thread for a ballroom dress she was working on. It wasn't till I was in the store that I realized I had not brought a sample with me. It was such a long walk back I decided to make my purchase without the sample. Since I was too small to see over the counter I put my hand up and banged on the glass case. When the saleslady leaned over and saw me I told her I wanted silk thread for a party dress.

"Where's your sample?" she said.

"I haven't one."

She thereupon walked around and picked me up in her arms and showed me the spools.

"I'll take that one," I said, and the thread matched the dress perfectly. Mother was so proud of me that day, and I wasn't exactly modest myself.

I shall never forget the time I tried to make Mother's cherished upright mahogany piano into pale pink. I wet the chalk in my mouth and then applied it to the piano. That would certainly have earned me a good spanking from the average mother, but my darling understood that I had wanted to surprise her with a new face of beauty. I am sure such a woman could be trusted to guide and instruct a child denied the privileges of public schooling.

What a joy my bicycle was to me! I used to save till I had ten cents and could rent a bicycle for an hour. Those were the moments, almost the only ones, when I was really a little girl. I remember so well the day Mother led me up to the window of a store and pointed to a bicycle. I was soon going to be eight years old.

"That's your birthday present, darling."

I was overwhelmed, but only for a moment, before my economical self came to the fore. I demanded to know how much it would cost. Mother said twenty-five dollars. I told her it was too expensive and flatly refused to accept it, but she assured me she could work out the problem. I suppose Mother should have been scolded for so indulging me, but was it indulgence? There has never been an automobile, not even my Rolls-Royce, which gave me the feeling of pride I experienced when Mother and I bicycled down the street side by side.

When my sister Lottie was in her teens her heart was set on a white willow plume. Mother spent five dollars of her meager savings to indulge Lottie on her birthday. One of the ladies in the Chauncey Olcott company took Mother to task for this useless extravagance.

"I'm going to give my children every happiness that I possibly can while I'm still living," my mother replied. "The time will come when I'm not here, and where a willow plume will mean nothing to Lottie. Now it does."

That was the sort of Mother Charlotte Smith was. Is it any wonder that her children adored her?

3

Cissy Denver started a little series of roles in which I starred with the Valentine Company. After Eva in *Uncle Tom's Cabin* I did little Willie in *East Lynne,* the baby in *Bootles' Baby,* and finally Mabel Payne in *The Little Red Schoolhouse.* This last production changed the course of my life. The writer of the play, Hal Reid, father of the famous motion-picture actor Wallace Reid, had come to Toronto to try out the play and while he was there he engaged all four of us Smiths for the Broadway performance. We would receive word in the fall when we should come to New York. Mother hurriedly sold all our furniture. Every preparation was made for a permanent removal to "the States," where, we had always been assured, the streets were paved with gold.

September and October passed . . . and still no word from Mr. Reid. Mother now suspected something had gone amiss, and when December rolled around she knew it. It wasn't till much later in New York that we learned what had happened.

c

Hal Reid had sold the play to a New York producer and apparently forgot completely the commitment he had made to the Smith clan of Toronto. Chuckie and I were especially put out by the waiting because we adored the play. She was my little boy friend Johnny Watson and I can still remember two or three of the lines. "Mabel," says Johnny, "do you like chicken?" And when Mabel replies, "Of course I do," Johnny, crooking his arm for her, says, "Well, take a wing."

It seems that *The Little Red Schoolhouse* had gone on the road in September, and in my role of Mabel Payne was a very beautiful little girl by the name of Lillian Gish. Lillian was traveling in the care of a very close friend of Mrs. Gish. When this woman fell ill and was obliged to return to New York for an operation, Lillian had to resign. That was in Buffalo. Somebody in the cast must have remembered the Smiths, for they then wired Mother, "We want Gladys—only Gladys." To which Mother promptly replied:

"If you want Gladys, you'll have to take Lottie, Jack, and Mother too."

They must have been in desperate need of a little girl for the role, because they gave in and hired the four of us at the aggregate sum of twenty dollars a week. Mother understudied all of the adult female roles; Lottie understudied Johnny Watson—the part she had originated in Toronto; and Jack and Lottie appeared in the schoolhouse scene. The play had now been renamed *For a Human Life*. On that twenty dollars a week Mother saved enough money to buy a Tailor Trunk—the prize possession of all professional people at that time. I still have that trunk. The die was cast, and Mother was resolved to follow through on a thoroughly professional basis. While we

In "The Little Red Schoolhouse"

were playing our one-night stands in *For a Human Life*, we
went from Buffalo to New York.

What a disappointment New York was to me! The great
sight in those days was the Flatiron Building; I remember how
unimpressed I was when I first saw it. And how I loathed New
York's theatrical boardinghouses! One of the more celebrated
houses of the time was "Mom Barrow's." When we four Smiths
took rooms there we knew we were really in show business. I
must confess, however, that I was never popular with Mom
Barrow herself. I remember how, one morning, at nine o'clock,
without knocking she burst into the room and shouted, "You'll
be down in five minutes or no breakfast!"

People of the theater do not rise early. Shocked into sudden
wakefulness, I said nothing, but the expression on my face must
have given more than a hint of my feelings. I learned later from
Mother that Mom Barrow had come up to her quivering with
rage and said, "Mrs. Smith, I like little Lottie and Johnny, but
as for Gladys, she's a fresh kid."

We had to learn our table manners all over again in New
York. So that we would not be conspicuous, Mother promptly
taught us the American way of changing our fork back
and forth instead of keeping it in the left as do the Canadians
and the English. Mother always wanted us to appear at our
best. Night after night we would stay up to wash and iron our
dresses "in consideration," as she put it, "first of ourselves
and second of others." She was also a great stickler in the
etiquette of gloves. I have never forgotten her pronouncement
on the subject:

"No lady ever went out without gloves. A real lady merits
the title when she puts her gloves on in the house. A lady isn't

so much of a lady when she puts them on on the stoop of her house. And a lady is no lady at all when she puts them on in the street."

Mother, of course, had come to New York on a very practical errand: to apply for the next season's work. The intensive and discouraging job hunt that now began laid the pattern for recurring years of pavement-pounding. No one can have an idea of what this means who has not personally looked for work on the stage. The motley crews of the fly-by-night theatrical companies of those days; the merciless summer heat of New York; the rudeness of the receptionists; the sight of starving actors with their celluloid collars and brave faces; the overly bleached blondes with their inevitable turquoise jewelry and one lingering piece of soiled finery, like a blouse or jabot, and the lip rouge that would begin to wear off as the heat grew and the day lengthened. The picture of Mother, Lottie, Johnny, and me trudging along to these offices will stay with me to my dying day. And later came the terrifying uncertainty of the nightly attendance.

All my life I have dreamed two recurring dreams, both nightmarish with dread. One of them involved an empty theater. To this day I have that dream before any sort of journey or project I may be embarking on. I seem to gauge the scope of the disaster ahead by the endless rows of empty seats. While the dream varies in some details, I am always on the stage when the curtain goes up. And always there is that unpeopled hollow before me, and the certainty that the play is a failure and the company will pack up and go home.

In the other nightmare I am again on the stage. This time I have forgotten my lines. I stand there speechless in the growing horror of my humiliation. I suppose deep down in me I fear being unprepared, unrehearsed, for what tomorrow may bring.

I have never really lost my nervousness of the theater, or of the camera, or of any public appearance, for that matter. I don't remember ever stepping before a camera without a certain anxiety. Often I would have chills and run a temperature for the first three or fours days, whether it was a play or a movie. That still happens to me before making a speech. I have always been hounded by this lack of confidence in myself. And I should like to say, emphatically and without exception, that I never liked any one of my pictures in its entirety. Once, in Pasadena, at the preview of one of my pictures and to the amazement of the entire company including myself, I suddenly heard my voice saying, out loud, "I wish to apologize for this picture and for my performance. I think they are both inexcusably bad." It seems that as the lights went on, they had called for a speech, I had jumped to my feet, and, like an automaton, I made that impulsive little speech. I was never so filled with remorse, because I had hurt the director and members of the cast.

To go back to my childhood. Mother finally signed us all up with Sullivan, Harris, and Woods for a famous play of the time called *The Fatal Wedding*. Since work was not to begin till the fall, we returned to Toronto to get through the long summer months as best we could with almost no funds. We had a rooster, I remember, which we all came to love as if it were another member of the family. It was kept in the back yard of the house

70

where Mother had rented our rooms in Toronto. We had not eaten a good meal for a long time, and suddenly, one day, as if out of nowhere, chicken appeared on the table. I glanced at the window that opened on the back yard. No one said a word, and no one so much as touched the chicken. When we had finished our dinner, such as it was, my brother Jack flung himself down on the bed and wept bitterly. To add to our woes, Mother came down with an illness that required surgery. It was performed in our rooms—we couldn't afford a hospital. During her operation I rocked myself in abject misery on the pedal of the sewing machine. I was in terror that I would now lose my mother as well as my father. Twenty-fours hours later we were on the train for New York. Ordinarily Mother should have spent two weeks in the hospital, followed by a period of convalescence.

How she survived that journey sitting up all night on the train I shall never know. We arrived next morning just in time to report to rehearsal. There was no time for breakfast.

The director of *The Fatal Wedding* was a cruel, pompous individual who delighted in crucifying those under his supervision. He snapped at Mother, "You'll have to do better than that or I'll replace you." Those words lashed me. Mother was able to whisper that none of us had eaten since the day before, that she would do better when she had had a cup of tea.

"I promise I'll be much better at rehearsal this afternoon," she pleaded.

I was the only one of the children to realize fully what Mother was going through at that moment. I knew that she was in pain, weak, tired, and frightened, that the whole uncertain future of the Smith family hung on the outcome of this cruel day.

71

BABY GLADYS SMITH

The Little Mother   In The Fatal Wedding Co
FRANK WENDT, Photo Artist,   Boonton, N. J.

72

I can still see the mean expression on that director's face at another rehearsal soon after. In the role of an Irish maid named Bridget, Mother was supposed to be carrying a bowl of flowers in one scene.

"And what would you have us suppose you are carrying there, Mrs. Smith," he sneered, "a piece of Limburger cheese?"

The first performance of *The Fatal Wedding* was a one-night stand in Pottsville, Pennsylvania. Mother had the opening lines. Just a few moments before she was to speak I grabbed Lottie and Johnny, and the three of us fell on our knees in a dark corner of the wings and prayed to God.

"Please, God," we said, "don't let Mama forget her lines." We were now afraid that God might punish Mother for telling fibs, as she had stated to the producer that she had played many parts, but the truth was that she had never really acted before in her life. Mother herself hated a liar worse than a thief; she used to say, "You can lock from a thief, but never from a liar."

Convinced that God would never overlook this great sin of Mother's, we remained on our knees for as long as she was on the stage, crying and praying. While we prayed to God, we kept one ear cocked to the stage. I remember we took turns going out to overhear Mother, and then hurrying back with a panting report and falling down on our knees again.

At eight

4

I was the star of *The Fatal Wedding,* a fact that
the publicity man sedulously brought home to
both the public and me. Garish handbills of magenta and bright
orange, reading " 'The Fatal Wedding' with Baby Gladys Smith
Is a Wonder," were thrown around the streets and deposited
in doorways. One day I got hold of one of these cards
and took what it said very seriously indeed. I began to think
of myself as a very important person, indispensable, in fact.
This new self-esteem grew. One evening Mother and I entered
the star dressing room of a theater on our route. The room was
in a frightful state of disorder. "I've never seen such dirt in
my life," Mother said. As for me, I put my hands on my hips
and exclaimed:

"The idea of expecting me, the star, to dress in a filthy place
like this. I simply won't go on tonight."

Mother had pinned a towel around her and was already
cleaning up the dressing table. She fastened an eagle eye on

me in the mirror. I had never seen and never again saw such an incredulous look on her face. She straightened up slowly and turned to face me.

"I want that speech repeated," she announced gravely.

With considerably less gusto and no self-confidence I repeated it.

"I'm grateful for one thing," said Mother. "That no one in the company heard you. You're not the star of the company! You're nothing but a naughty, spoiled, swell-headed little upstart."

I hung my head in shame and said nothing.

"That I should have lived to hear such a revolting speech from the mouth of my own daughter," Mother went on. "I've suspected this for some time. In fact, I've seen it in your performance lately. You're quite right about one thing: you are *not* going on tonight. Lottie will take your part. You are not going on until you can learn humility and behave yourself like any normal nice little child."

It was the greatest punishment Mother had ever administered to me; it cut me more than a thousand whips.

"Now, Gladys," Mother went on, "you can go find a pail and a mop and a broom and help me clean up this dressing room."

From that moment to this I have been in such terror of having it said that I had a swelled head that I'm afraid I have often gone to the other extreme.

Nineteen weeks of one-night stands of *The Fatal Wedding*, averaging eight and nine performances a week, including matinees—never sleeping twice in the same bed! What hectic weeks they were for the Widow Smith and her three children,

76

Johnny aged five, Lottie aged seven, and Gladys aged eight. Mother was always washing and packing and sewing. When she could, and the facilities were at hand, she would make clothes for all of us. One of my most cherished memories during those bustling weeks is of Mother sitting up in the middle of the night making new dresses for Lottie and me. Mother was so facile with her hands she even learned to make fur coats for us, buying the skins and stretching them herself.

While we were on the road, often rushing out of the hotel in the wee small hours to catch the next train, Mother had all she could do to keep us awake. One morning she devised a little game. Bringing us all sharply to attention, she announced that we would be a German band, she carrying the main theme, I the "oompah" part, and Johnny and Chuckie filling in as they saw fit. Tired and sleepy as we were, the trick worked. Like rigid little toy soldiers, we marched down the hotel stairs, along the street, and over to the station into the train. But one morning, Johnny, the family sleepyhead, rebelled. It was three o'clock and we had to catch one of those awful milk trains for our next one-night stand.

"We've got to get up, Johnny," said Mother.

But Johnny went skittering across the big wide bed and curled up against the wall. "I'm so sleepy, Mama," he said; "I want to stay here. I don't want to go."

That was one of the few times I ever saw Mother very close to the breaking point. I knew it tore at her heart to force sleepy-eyed little Johnny to dress and go out into that cold night and onto that musty, uncomfortable train. She sat down and cried, whereupon Lottie and I went after Jack and, in double-quick time, put on his long-ribbed cotton stockings. Seeing Mother cry had sobered us into determined action. But that wasn't the end of it. In the middle of our marching game, with all the imitated brass effects, Johnny revolted again. He planted his foot in the snow and said:

"I won't go, Mama. I want to go back home to bed; I'm too sleepy."

Mother coaxed and pleaded and promised him a top, or whatever his heart was set on, if only he would be a sport and make one more effort. To no avail. Johnny stood his ground and said, "I won't go!" Mother was carrying both her suitcase and his, while Lottie and I carried our own. There was a very low iron railing where Johnny had stopped. Mother determinedly dropped the two bags on the sidewalk and walked back the few steps to Johnny. Without a word she picked him up and threw him over that railing into a deep, soft bed of snow. That was the only moment in my life that I actually disliked my mother. I was too young to realize that she was using drastic methods because the situation was drastic. Our livelihood depended on our catching that train; even more important, it meant that the four of us would remain together. Mother stubbornly marched on, Lottie and I, torn between her and Johnny, following disconsolately behind. I turned my head, and to my great relief I saw my brother scramble out of the snow and call out, "Mama, don't leave me!" Lottie and I broke rank and dashed back to Johnny, and when we again caught up with Mother, tears were silently streaming down four faces in the cold early morning air.

For years I couldn't bear the color crimson and the reason was the heavy red upholstery of the day coaches that always smelled of coal dust. Mother would stretch us out on the seats with the iron rests and lie awake herself. The train would slowly fill up as it stopped at all the little villages of the milk route. I would awaken three or four hours later with my feet on top of the radiator and my shoes fairly bursting with the heat. I learned to sleep sitting up, even standing up. In our fondest dreams we never knew the luxury of a Pullman berth. Anything was improvised for a pillow, from a suitcase to a fat roll of newspapers. Our breakfast generally consisted of stale ham sandwiches left over from the day before, and a glass of ice water. Since those days I've heard actors complain about the most trivial inconveniences. On such occasions I wonder even more at the unbelievable courage of Charlotte Pickford Hennessey Smith.

Mother was a very beautiful woman and could easily have married again; but she never did. She used to confide in me as if I were a grownup. Each of the successive suitors would be given a thorough going-over, and we would have many a good laugh over the peculiarities of their approach. Of course Chuckie, Johnny, and I were secretly haunted by the fear that someday Mother might change her attitude and give us a new father. Without Mother's knowing it a conspiracy was under way to thwart any likely contender's chance for Mother's hand. I remember one very attractive fellow, with a strong cockney accent, by the name of Jones. At his first appearance we knew instinctively that this was just about the strongest competition we would ever have to face. The three of us got together and took decisive action. While Mr. Jones was visiting Mother one day, we marched in and out of the room singing a little cockney jingle: "Little Papsy Wapsy, Chickapidee Chum, Ochi, Pochi,

Chim." It made no sense at all, but it drove Mother's Mr. Jones nearly crazy. Whatever ardor he might have had suddenly fled —and he along with it—at the thought of what lay in store for him as the Widow Smith's second husband.

I shall never forget Mr. Jones's exit—the tall, thin figure, spluttering with embarrassment and rage, clumsily hurrying to get out of the front room and making himself only more awkward and ridiculous as he did so. Mother tried to be cross with us and discipline us after the routing of Mr. Jones, but she too joined in the merriment when the front door had finally slammed shut on her latest beau. Her only comment to me was, "Gladys, your cockney accent is abominable; we'll have to do something about it."

Among her many talents Mother had a way of making anything edible go a long way. I remember how she would put a round steak on the breadboard and beat it with a rolling pin till it was tender. There was a specialty of hers that we hungrily called "heavenly hash." How she made it I never found out, but hash is my favorite dish to this day. Mother never threw away any of the water from the vegetables. Even the juice from the tinned vegetables was carefully preserved. She would add flour and butter to them, a pinch of salt and pepper, perhaps a little milk or cream, and the result was delicious, nourishing, filling, and inexpensive.

In illness Mother was an unfailing source of comfort. There were one hundred and one remedies in the home book of medicine that she carried around in her head—a legacy of generations that had gone before her. Mother used goose grease and meal and red onions to reduce the poisons in the body. I used to watch her in awe as she applied this weird concoction to the soles of my feet, the palms of my hands, under my arms, and around my throat.

"Mrs. Smith," said the doctor one day after observing a change for the better in me, "are you doing something other than what I prescribed? I can't understand why the child's throat isn't swollen and is still so supple."

Somewhat guiltily Mother explained what she had done.

"Well, I don't know"—the doctor hesitated—"but I see no harm in keeping it up."

When Lottie once went to a hospital with typhoid fever, Mother remained with her for ten long weeks till she was better. The nurses and sisters gave up trying to persuade my sister to eat something. It was only Mother who could make Lottie eat, and the doctor later said she owed her life to Mother's nursing.

5

I shall never forget the first time Lottie and I were separated from Mother. We were engaged for a play called *The Child Wife,* and this required our parting from both Johnny and Mother. I can still remember the loneliness of being without them in so many different cities and on so many train trips.

Before consenting to our going without her Mother had arranged with the stage manager to have a married couple in the company see to it that Lottie and I got to and from the theater safely. The couple were childless. And we soon found out they had no love for children. They avoided us as much as they possibly could. By the time we reached Baltimore we had decided not to consult them about anything. This meant we had to do some quick thinking. It was around three in the morning when we arrived and we had no lodging. When the entire company boarded a streetcar to go up to the center of town, Lottie and I slumped into two seats at the rear. As the trolley moved on I looked out the window and watched the signs along the way. When I spotted what looked like a suitable hotel, I nudged Lottie and told the conductor to stop. We slipped off the streetcar unnoticed by the other members of the company. The "Four Cohans" were playing opposite that hotel, and perhaps that was why I chose it.

The hotel was a sort of saloon on the street level, with room accommodations on the floors above. The bar was closed when we rang the bell, but the lights were still on. After a few moments of silence a mountain of a man, encased in a huge white apron, came to the door, and in mixed Anglo-German asked what we wanted.

"We are professional people, sir," I said, "and we would like to engage a room."

"Vair is de mutter?" he asked.

"We are traveling alone, sir."

"*Ganz allein?*" he said. "*Gott in Himmel!* Two babies yet!"

From the dark interior beyond him he called out his equally substantial wife, who immediately took charge of us. While her husband went off to prepare a supper of warm milk and bread for us, she put hot-water bags in our bed. It was Christmas Eve, and what followed was a week of paradise for Lottie and me, darkened only by the thought of Mother and Jack being so far away. This German couple gave us all the love and protection we needed for our one week in Baltimore. They saw to it that every day we got to the theater and back safely. No one in the company ever inquired what was happening to us, because, I suppose, they assumed we were being looked after by the childless couple.

My salary during that engagement was twenty-five dollars a

84

week. To make it seem more, I would change every five-dollar bill into one-dollar bills and stuff them into a chamois "boodle-bag" I wore around my neck.

It was during that first night in Baltimore that Lottie and I decided we had to do something about the money, now totaling sixty-eight dollars. Many of those remaining hours of Christmas Eve we spent discussing the dangers to which our great riches were exposed. We were frankly worried about the saloon below. Christmas morning Lottie and I gave over to hiding and then retrieving the bundle of bills. The next day, after a whispered conference, we took our boodlebag to the post office and sent Mother a money order for the full contents.

This was the beginning of what was to be a pattern of separation for the whole family. Mother called these leave-takings "partings on the road." They were nightmares for her, and the season following *The Child Wife* she was determined that we should all be together again.

The four of us hustled down to lower Broadway to apply for work at the office of a man named August Depeux, manager of none other than Chauncey Olcott, one of the bigwigs of the theater at that time. Olcott was Irish and practically everyone in his company was Irish too.

As we entered Mr. Depeux's office, the three of us, Jack, Lottie, and I, scrunched down in our clothes to appear as small as possible, the idea being that if they wanted us taller we could always straighten up. To our great disappointment we learned that they wanted two big boys and one little girl for the roles of Lord Bertie, Lord Algernon, and Lady Phyllis in a play called *Edmund Burke*, which was to be a sumptuous production, complete with brocades and satins. Mother, however, was so convincing in her claim that we could do the three roles that, to our great jubilation, we were engaged. Of course her soft brogue did no harm either.

Lottie played two parts in *Edmund Burke*, doubling as Pat, a little Irish peasant boy and Lord Algernon. Jack played Lady Phyllis, and I played Lord Bertie. You would have had to know Jack to realize what a comedown and utter humiliation it was for him to have to play the part of a girl. I would have to beg, coax, and cajole him to put on his wig, the long pantalets, the brocaded pannier dress over a satin skirt, and the voluminous organdy petticoats. The insult of insults, of course, was the pantalets. I would go on using all my powers of persuasion till the very minute the performance was scheduled to start.

Jack would finally give in, but to show his defiance, the minute he got off the stage he would lift his skirts right up over his head as he climbed the stairs to his dressing room, and show his long pantalets. I could always read the shock on the faces of the stagehands, who at first didn't know that he was a boy.

My own performance as Lord Bertie was apparently satisfactory, because a year later I again found myself hired for a male role. It was the part of a little Irish boy, Patsy Poore, in a play called *In Convict Stripes*. The manager told Mother that I would have to cut off my long curls for the part. Mother flatly refused, and was gathering me up to leave, when the manager suggested that I could have my curls if I agreed to wear a wig. Mother agreed to that. I had nothing to say about it, since to the very last day she lived her word was law. Mother, took Lottie and Jack back to Canada to put them in school, and I went on tour as quite a top-heavy Patsy Poore. I wore a bright red wig, and with all that hair concealed under it my head was the size of a very large pot.

6

Before leaving me behind in New York for the rehearsals of *In Convict Stripes* Mother had again to find someone to take care of me. This time the lady's name was Jean Patriquin, an ex-schoolteacher from San Francisco who was the villainess of the show. I was introduced to my future protectress at a theater on 107th Street, where we went for rehearsal. My only recollection of that first meeting was that we took an instant dislike to one another. When we later got over our first impressions, she told me that after we were introduced, her husband asked her what I was like. "A typical theatrical brat, blond curls and all," was her reply. I told her, in turn, that when Mother asked me what I thought of Miss Patriquin, I said, "A very cross-looking lady, and I don't think she likes children."

It wasn't long before we became fast friends, and have been to this day. What an arduous season that was! Without Mother, to begin with. Then the dirty theaters. And to top it, the unruly gallery audiences. I remember how exasperated I was the first time this sudden and crude shouting and stamping erupted in my face. I soon found a device that worked like magic: I would stand with my back turned to the gallery, with an occasional black look in that direction, till the hullabaloo died down. During this tour Miss Patriquin became my self-appointed tutor. I had been carrying my own schoolbooks with me on the road. Miss Patriquin carefully looked them over and advised my finding newer and more progressive ones. This I did, and the two of us would pore over them, page by page, as the train raced on to our next performance of *In Convict Stripes*.

It was about this time that I made up my mind, as firmly and decisively as I could, that I would land on Broadway or give up the theater for good. I was then thirteen years of age. As I had it figured out, I would spend the two summer weeks looking for work on Broadway, and I was also determined that it was to be tops only. That failing, I was going to ask a kind Irish family named Whelan, our neighbors in our last family reunion in New York, whether I could board with them. I learned that I could earn five dollars a week ripping out basting threads in a dressmaking establishment. My idea was to work during the day and go to school at night to learn design, with the ultimate aim, in the not too distant future, of setting up my own factory. I had no intention of putting all my hopes in one basket!

While my beloved family was still in Canada, I went to live with the Whelans—Minnie, her sister Kate, and two nephews. Then I began the familiar vigil of waiting and searching. Flight after flight of stairs; mile upon mile of hot, sticky pavement—and all this time, night after night, in the Whelans' tiny railroad flat, immaculately clean and orderly, I slept on a Morris chair, with the back let down and an overstuffed chair at my feet to provide as comfortable a makeshift bed as possible. There aren't many families that would take in a growing girl with remuneration, let alone without, but the Whelans were a truly Christian family.

One day I read in the papers that Blanche Bates was playing in David Belasco's *The Girl of the Golden West* in a theater in Brooklyn. I immediately decided on a bold course of action. David Belasco was one of the two producers I had set up as my goal to meet.

That evening I took the subway to Brooklyn, told the stage doorman I had to see Miss Bates. "I'll call her colored maid, miss," he said. It was intermission time between the second and third acts. When the maid came out, I explained that I wanted Miss Bates to give me a letter to Mr. Belasco asking him to see me. It was not till long after that I learned from Blanche Bates herself how it was only because of this kind Negro girl's plea on my behalf that she consented to allow me to use her name. "No," she had said at first, "I won't see anyone; I'm just too tired." But the maid persisted. "I've never asked you to do me a favor in all the years I have worked for you," she said. "But I ask you now. Please, Miss Bates, send that little girl with the curls to see Mr. Belasco. I know you'd feel the way I do, if you saw her." Miss Bates relented. "All right, tell her to say to Mr. Belasco that I sent her, but don't bother me any more about it."

I had been up to Mr. Belasco's offices in the Republic Building every Monday morning. Promptly at ten I would be sent away with all the other actors and told to come back the following Monday morning at ten. I had no idea what play Mr. Belasco was planning to stage the coming season, and as he produced only one play a year, there was one chance in a hundred that he would need a child actress. This time I did not wait for Monday. The following morning, fortified by Miss Bates's message, I marched up several flights of stairs to Mr. Belasco's office, only to be stopped by the office boy. I delivered Miss Bates's message. But the office boy wouldn't budge. And as my voice grew insistent, a door opened, and William Dean, who was then Mr. Belasco's manager, put out his head and said, "What's all this rumpus about? Let the little girl come in."

The moment I entered Mr. Dean's office, I cried out, "My life depends on seeing Mr. Belasco!" This must have amused and impressed him, as no doubt did Miss Bates's message, because after a few more weeks of nervous waiting I received word to be in the lobby of the theater after the performance on a certain night.

The play was *Rose of the Rancho*, with Frances Starr in the leading role. Minnie Whelan accompanied me on that fateful night. When the theater let out, we walked into the lobby and waited. Finally Mr. Belasco appeared. I watched him approach, overawed by the priestly attire, long, curly white hair, heavy black brows, and the sharpest, loveliest eyes I had ever seen on man or woman. When he was standing before us I couldn't lift my eyes to him.

"What's your name?" he asked right off.

"At home in Toronto, I'm Gladys Smith; but on the road I'm Gladys Milbourne Smith."

This struck him very funny, though he tried to conceal his amusement.

"We'll have to find another name for you. What are some of the other names in your family?"

I told him.

"Key, Bolton, De Beaumont, Kirby, Pickford . . ."

"Pickford it is. Is Gladys your only name? Haven't you another?"

"I was baptized Gladys Marie. . . ."

"Well, my little friend, from now on your name will be Mary Pickford, and will you come back, please, with your aunt, tomorrow night and see our play?"

After a pause he added, "Be prepared to give me a sample of your acting."

I was speechless with joy and excitement. Mr. Belasco had turned to go when he faced me again.

"By the way, what made you say your life depended on seeing me?"

"Well, you see, Mr. Belasco, I'm thirteen years old, and I think I'm at the crossroads of my life. I've got to make good between now and the time I'm twenty, and I have only seven years to do it in. Besides, I'm the father of my family and I've got to earn all the money I can."

"I see," he said dubiously. "But why all the hurry?"

"Mr. Belasco," I said, looking straight up into his face now, "I made up my mind that if I couldn't appear in a Broadway play this fall I would give up the theater forever."

I could see that stifled glint of amusement again.

"What made you pick me?"

"Well, Mother always says I should aim high or not at all."

"Hmm . . . And who else had you chosen?"

"Mr. Charles Frohman."

"Have you seen him yet?"

"No, sir," I said. "I wanted to see you first."

Mr. Belasco left us, and as we started out of the theater, I asked "Aunt" Minnie, as I called her, whether she would mind, late though it was, walking the twenty blocks back to the apartment. I was in too exalted a state to ride a streetcar.

The next night "Aunt" Minnie and I came to witness the performance of *Rose of the Rancho*. We waited in the box assigned to us until the audience left the theater and the set had been cleared away. Mr. Belasco came to the box and, grasping my hand, led me onto the stage.

"Would you like any props?"

"I would like a chair, sir, to represent a policeman."

I apologized to Mr. Belasco for the poor dialogue, saying it was the only scene I knew, but that since I hadn't had time to study anything else, I hoped he would realize that the lines were from a very melodramatic play.

Mr. Belasco merely nodded from a seat in the front row of the orchestra and signaled me to begin. "Aunt" Minnie, the only other spectator, was concealed behind the velvet curtains of the stage box. The scene was where Patsy Poore pleads with the policeman not to arrest him because his poor old blind mother is totally dependent upon him. With nothing to aid me but a kitchen chair, and the cold, cruel light of the pilot lamp I proceeded to give a "sample" of my acting. When I reached the last line of my monologue I closed my mouth and stood there ice-cold and trembling. Mr. Belasco climbed up on the stage and took my two hands in his.

"So you want to be an actress, little girl?"

94

"No, sir," I replied without hesitation; "I have been an actress. I want to be a good actress now."

There was again that hint of suppressed merriment in his face.

"Would you like to meet a *good* actress?"

"Oh yes, sir!"

"Well, then, come with me!"

Mr. Belasco led me by the hand and knocked on the door of a dressing room.

"Frances," he said, when it opened, "here's a young lady who wants to be a good actress like you."

Graciously Miss Starr answered, "That will not be difficult, my little dear. Under the Maestro's guiding hand I know that you will go far."

I looked around the star's dressing room, and something inside of me whispered, "One day this dressing room will be yours, silver star and all." That night Mr. Belasco offered me a role in his next production, *The Warrens of Virginia.* My first thought on leaving the theater was of Mother. I hadn't said one word to her of my recent decisions. For one thing I knew it would not be an easy matter to get her approval of my night-school and dress-designing idea if my theatrical hopes fell through. Aunt Minnie permitted me to stay up long enough to write Mother in Toronto. My letter contained just two lines, inscribed in big black letters right across the top of the page:

GLADYS SMITH NOW MARY PICKFORD ENGAGED BY
DAVID BELASCO TO APPEAR ON BROADWAY THIS FALL

Mr. Belasco had decided to give me the role of Betty, the younger daughter of *The Warrens of Virginia.* The play was written by William de Mille, whose brother Cecil B. de Mille was one of the cast. Charlotte Walker, Frank Keenan, and that gifted actress Emma Dunn were also in the play. My part, among other things, called for a Southern accent, which I tried to master by listening to the genuine Southern speech of Miss Walker and Mr. Keenan.

I enjoyed a small triumph one day when the mother of William and Cecil de Mille, a southerner herself, asked me what part of the South I came from.

Not long after rehearsals started I had my first taste of David Belasco in action. Things had been moving along smoothly enough, with only an occasional waspish comment about a detail of diction or acting, till one night I was brought sharply to attention by a loud and commanding voice. We had worked far into the night. I was half asleep in a stage box, waiting for the second act. The set was a stately dining room of one of the old Virginia mansions, authentic in every detail from the rugs and antiques down to the crystal and silver molasses container. Mr. Belasco couldn't bear cheap imitations. Suddenly his voice boomed out:

"Hold everything!"

I sat bolt upright, my eyes and ears jolted into wakeful suspense.

Mr. Belasco climbed up on the stage and elaborately stalked the molasses jar. Everyone froze. Mr. Belasco adjusted his glasses and leafed through the manuscript in his hand. Then he reached for a spoon and tasted the contents of the molasses

In "The Warrens of Virginia"

jar. In evident disgust he flung down the spoon, and with the roar of a lion called for the property man.

"Taste that!" commanded Mr. Belasco.

The property man dipped a spoon into the thick fluid and brought it to his lips.

"What is it?" bellowed the Maestro.

"Maple syrup, sir."

"And if you please, what does the manuscript call for?"

"Molasses, sir."

"And you dare waste my time and the time of the ladies and gentlemen of my company with maple syrup?"

With that he dashed the jar into a thousand pieces on the floor, and began to jump up and down on the sticky mess, thereby driving it deeper and deeper into the beautiful Oriental rug. When at length his fury was spent, he ordered the property man to clean up the stage, and gave one last shout:

"Never, never presume to take such liberties with me again!"

Mr. Belasco suddenly made a sticky beeline for the box where I was seated in frozen immobility. I tried to copy Alice in Wonderland by making myself as small as possible, but to no avail. Mr. Belasco looked at me with twinkling eyes and asked:

"Betty, tell me, what did you think of my performance?"

And all I could mutter in reply was, "I—I—I don't think I understand, s-s-sir."

"This is a great secret between you and me," he said in mock confidence. "I find it absolutely necessary to break something at least once before opening night in order to keep the cast on their toes."

What a merciless stickler for detail Mr. Belasco was I soon

learned at my own expense. The night of the dress rehearsal it was my turn to incur his wrath. My costume in the role of the daughter of the impoverished Warren family was a faded cotton rose tablecloth which had been washed to pale pink, and beneath that the pet wardrobe aversion of the Smith family, pantalets. I remember I heard Mr. Belasco call out, in that imperious voice of his, "Where is Betty?" Little Betty was brought out on the stage in all her faded finery. Mr. Belasco surveyed me for a few moments.

"There's something wrong with her costume," he said, and after a studious pause, "I know, I know!" And, in a monstrous growl, "Where are her pantalets?"

The wardrobe mistress was rushed out to face the erupting volcano. "Mr. Belasco, I put them on Betty myself," she said quivering. Those flashing, piercing eyes were back on my costume.

"What have you done with them?" he asked gravely.

With that the wardrobe mistress pulled up my dress and pulled down the rolled-up legs of my pantalets. This was a thousand times worse than what I had tried to avoid, for now it drew everybody's attention to me and to the hated unmentionables. I was embarrassed almost beyond endurance. But I said nothing. To me David Belasco was like the King of England, Julius Caesar, and Napoleon all rolled into one.

Before we opened on Broadway, we were four weeks on the road with *The Warrens of Virginia,* our first stop being Boston early in the fall of 1907. Mr. Belasco spent the entire four weeks with us, polishing and perfecting the dialogue as we moved from city to city.

On a Monday night in November, 1907, the *Warrens of Vir-*

ginia opened in New York City. I had reached the goal I set for myself: I was actually on Broadway in a Belasco production.

What a magnificent sight it was from the stage in those days! The women wore gorgeous evening gowns and the men were always in formal attire, their white shirts and waistcoats gleaming in the dimness. And I shall never forget the wave of perfume that wafted across the footlights to us on the stage. How happily we all basked in it! What a far cry from the grimy atmosphere of *In Convict Stripes!*

A long and successful engagement of *The Warrens of Virginia* followed, and in the fall of 1908 we were on the road again, with a much longer and more arduous itinerary.

During this engagement I was making thirty dollars a week, and I tried to live on ten dollars. I did my own laundry, both my street dresses and my theater wardrobe. That was nothing new, however. I had always traveled with a small washboard and an electric iron.

It was in Chicago, while touring with *The Warrens* that I had my first taste of the "flickers." The makeshift movie house was a long, narrow store on State Street, outfitted with train and streetcar seats. The camera was mounted on an engine that sped through tunnels and around tracks. The illusion of actually being on a train was so vivid that I became violently carsick. This gave me a horror of the "flickers," and I vowed never to go back. Not Lottie and Jack, however. They became hopeless addicts of the new fad very early, and I remember beseeching Mother to keep them away from this fearful iniquity. Every time they could raise five or ten cents, they would rush off to a store on West Twenty-third Street to see a film.

In the spring 1909, when *The Warrens of Virginia* ended its

100

run, we were all reunited in New York. I had saved about $200 and Mother and Lottie also had some money from touring—this time in *Rugged Robin* with Chauncey Olcott. For a while we managed to pay for rent and food and even indulged in one wonderful clothes splurge. As the weeks went by and our funds got lower, however, the old sense of insecurity returned to plague us. We knew we must find work, and yet finding work would probably separate us once more.

It was occasions like this that made me more resolved than ever that my family would someday know real security. I never for a moment doubted that I myself would ultimately provide it for them. My confidence in our future wealth seemed so exaggerated that everyone made a kind of joke of it.

I remember one slushy afternoon when my cousin Mabel (one of Aunt Lizzie's daughters) and I were waiting for a streetcar at Forty-second Street and Seventh Avenue. A chauffeur-driven limousine carrying two conspicuously rich women rolled past, splashing mud all over Mabel's best dress and my only one. Mabel was furious.

"Why do we have to ride in a dirty streetcar when other people go around in glass bird cages like that!" she cried. "We're every bit as good as they are and a darn sight prettier."

"Never mind, Mabel," I told her soothingly; "we're going to have a car even nicer than that—and very soon, too."

Mabel's delicate rejoinder was: "Pardon me, Mrs. Astorbilt, your diamond tiara is slipping!"

It took me years to live down my casual remark about the car. Whenever Jack wanted to tease me he would seize a chair, and with ultrarefinement instruct Lottie to retire to the back seat so he could take the wheel.

101

Sometimes when I got home from work the two of them would rush to the window exclaiming, "Have you tied your Stanley Steamer to the lamppost?"

It wasn't till six years later, in 1913, that I had my moment of triumph. Mabel and I were again together on Seventh Avenue, not on a street corner waiting for a trolley, but luxuriously seated in my beautiful cream and gray Cadillac. As we came to the corner of Forty-second Street, Mabel grabbed my arm.

"Mary, do you remember that corner? You told me there that we would be driving in this very car someday!"

That particular spring after *The Warrens of Virginia* closed our funds got so low that Mother made what seemed to me a very shocking proposal.

"Would you be very much against applying for work at the Biograph Studios, Gladdie?" she said one day.

"Oh no, not that, Mama!"

"Well, now, it's not what I would want for you, either, dear. I thought if you could make enough money we could keep the family together. I'm sure it would make up for the lowering of our standard."

I wanted to argue with her, but I knew better. I agreed.

"I knew you would, dear," said Mother. "It's only to tide us over. They say the pay is good . . . and besides, I'll let you wear your first silk stockings and high-heeled shoes."

Maybe that as much as anything else decided me. The following morning, glorying in my new finery, I decide to walk from where we were living on West Seventeenth Street to Fourteenth Street, take a cross-town trolley, and in paying my fare

102

ask the conductor for a transfer up Broadway. I had no intention of wasting a perfectly good nickel. I alighted in front of
the Biograph and Bioscope Studios with the transfer clasped
firmly in my hand. I would step into this hated place, I told
myself, pay the promised call and get out as fast as I could. I
would then use my transfer to reach the legitimate-theater agen-
cies on Broadway, where I was convinced I belonged. I would
be able to say to Mother, honestly and truthfully, "I did what
you asked me to." In my secret heart I was disappointed in
Mother: permitting a Belasco actress, and her own daughter
at that, to go into one of those despised, cheap, loathsome
motion-picture studios. It was beneath my dignity as an artist,
which I most certainly considered myself at the time. Bellig-
erently I marched up the steps of Biograph.

Up to that time the family had always called me Gladys.
They had never taken the "Mary" business very seriously.
But on that March day of 1909, on East Fourteenth Street in
New York, Gladys was sent back to Canada and Mary Pick-
ford was to embark on a great and thrilling career.

7

As I crossed the marble-floored foyer of the old
mansion occupied by the Biograph Studio, a man
came through the swinging door opposite me and began to
look me over in a manner that was too jaunty and familiar for
my taste.

"Are you an actress?" he demanded at once.

"I most certainly am," I retorted.

"What, if any, experience have you had, may I ask?"

"Only ten years in the theater, sir, and two of them with
David Belasco," I said icily.

"You're too little and too fat, but I may give you a chance.
My name is Griffith. What's yours?"

The name meant nothing to me at all. I thought him a pompous and insufferable creature and I wanted more than ever to
escape. Instead I found myself being led through two swinging doors and into the ladies' dressing room. In passing I remember being overawed by the circular ballroom which had

David Ward Griffith

been converted into the studio proper. In the middle of the room were low-hanging Cooper-Hewitt banks of blue lights, giving a sinister and uncanny atmosphere to the place. No one paid the slightest attention to Mr. Griffith and me as we walked by. The dressing room was deserted. He sat me down and told me to wait.

Now I had heard about studios from older girls in our West Side neighborhood where I had roomed with Aunt Minnie and Aunt Kate. I had also heard, in hushed tones, about architect Stanford White's studio and a girl who had lived in the same street named Evelyn Nesbit. I was hastily tiptoeing out of the dressing room when Mr. Griffith reappeared. He told me that I was to be given a test, the first, and, I may add, the *only* test that I was ever subjected to at Biograph. It was for *Pippa Passes*, and Mr. Griffith himself put on my make-up.

The Biograph camera

*"The Female
of the Species"*

The result seemed more appropriate for Pancho Villa than for
Pippa. A makeshift costume was rounded up in the wardrobe
department—a tiny cellar alcove set aside for the Biograph
costume rack.

Wearing this grotesque make-up, I was led on the stage and,
without any introduction to the cast, given a quick briefing on
what I was to do. Then came my second shock of the day: I
heard the actors and actresses calling each other by their first
names. That I thought improper beyond belief. In the Belasco
company, and in the theater in general, I had heard people
addressed only by their surnames. I noticed, however, that no
one ever addressed the gentleman in the striped suit as anything but "Mr. Griffith."

To add to my worries, I was handed a guitar and told to
act as if I were singing and strumming!

During the filming of this scene in which everyone improvised his own lines, a handsome young man, with a melodious
Irish voice, stepped forth and nonchalantly said:

"Who's the dame?"

108

That was going too far. I forgot all about the guitar, the scene, my grotesque make-up, and Mr. Griffith, and turned the full force of my indignation on this boor.

"How dare you, sir, insult me? I'll have you understand I'm a perfectly respectable young girl, and don't you dare call me a bad name!"

With that Mr. Griffith let out a roar that would have done the M.G.M. lion credit.

"Miss . . . Miss . . . what the devil is your name? But no matter . . . Never, do you hear, never stop in the middle of a scene. Do you know how much film costs per foot? You've ruined it! Start from the beginning!"

In those days "dame" meant to me just one thing—a loose woman. I had just never heard a girl publicly referred to as "a dame." Of course that young Irishman had meant no offense and was simply ad-libbing as they all did in the early movies. Whatever his faults, obscene language in the presence of a lady was not one of them. I should know, because his name was Owen Moore, and he later became my first husband.

Why Mr. Griffith asked me to come back the next day is still a matter of amazement to me. I was positive this was the end of my career in the "flickers." I knew it in my heart. I put ten years in the theater, and I knew whether a performance was good or bad. Mine that day at the Biograph Studio was distinctly bad.

It was well past eight o'clock when I returned to the dressing room and removed my hated make-up. Mr. Griffith was waiting for me outside.

"Will you dine with me?"

"I'm sorry, Mr. Griffith, I've never dined with any boy, let alone a man, and besides I have to leave immediately for Brooklyn. My mother and sister are playing there with Mr. Olcott."

"Will you come back tomorrow? Our pay for everybody is five dollars a day. We pay only by the day."

Already my Scotch blood was coming to the fore.

"I'm a Belasco actress, Mr. Griffith, and I must have ten."

He laughed.

"Agreed! Five dollars for today and ten for tomorrow. But keep it to yourself. No one is paid that much, and there will be a riot if it leaks out."

It had begun to rain earlier and by now it was coming down in buckets. Mr. Griffith kindly accompanied me in the downpour with his umbrella, leaving me at the subway with the words, "Till tomorrow at nine sharp." I was wet through when I arrived at the theater in Brooklyn, as I had to walk several blocks. My brand-new high-heeled shoes were ruined, and so were my silk stockings. A $3.50 straw hat with a big dark blue satin bow was a sight for tears, and my beautiful $15 blue serge Easter suit was one wringing mess. When I opened the door of the dressing room the first thing I saw was Johnny, curled up like a little snail on top of a trunk, sound asleep. Lottie and Mother were on-stage. Shivering and soaking wet, I sat down and waited. Clutched in my hand was the wet five-dollar bill. That was how they saw me when the door opened. Mother gave a shriek and promptly set about removing my wet garments and putting them over the radiator, together with the dripping five-dollar bill.

"They're going to pay me ten dollars a day from tomorrow on, Mama," I told her, my teeth chattering.

110

"You see, I was right after all, dear," she said.

I didn't dare tell her how much I hated that awful place on Fourteenth Street.

The next morning, promptly at 7:30, an alarm clock shimmied off the table onto the floor of my bedroom. Sleepy and aching all over, I never was so reluctant to rise in my life. But I got to the studio at nine o'clock on the dot, walking all the way this time, to save the five cents. I remember praying that no one from the theater would see me going up the Biograph steps. That day I played a ten-year-old girl in a picture entitled *Her First Biscuits*. Shortly after I arrived at the studio Mr. Griffith called out to Linda Arvidson, to whom he was then secretly married:

"Linda, go over to Fifth Avenue and buy this child a linen and lace dress, size ten, and shoes, socks, and hat to match for the role she's going to play."

I learned later that to costume me for that one day's work had cost all of $10.50. If I had had any doubt before, I had absolutely none now that the picture industry was mad. I found the work less irksome that day, and before I knew it I was back in the dressing room removing my make-up and getting into my street clothes. I was going through the swinging doors into the foyer when Mr. Griffith called out to me.

"Will you play the lead tomorrow?"

"Why, yes, sir!"

"Do you know anything about love-making?"

After several inaudible gulps I assured him I did.

At that moment a carpenter passed by us, carrying a papier-mâché pillar.

Mr. Griffith asked him to set the pillar down.

111

"All right, Pickford, make love to that pillar."

I was fifteen years old. I had never gone on a date, much less been kissed by a boy. Hoping to escape, I said:

"Please, Mr. Griffith, how could I make love to a cold pillar?"

I had no sooner said that than Owen Moore stepped out of the men's dressing room.

"Come here, Moore!" Griffith shouted to him.

Moore walked over to us, a puzzled smile on his handsome Irish face.

"Stand there!" Mr. Griffith directed him. "Miss Pickford doesn't like to make love to a lifeless pillar. See if she can do any better with you."

Panic-stricken, I was ready to rebel and walk out on the whole sickening business, when I remember the ten dollars Mr. Griffith had promised me. I pulled myself together and tried to recall how I had seen people make love in the theater. I decided that the way to do it was to look lovingly into the man's eyes. I made up my mind right then and there that there would be no kissing. I had been taught to regard kissing in public as vulgar in the extreme and completely unnecessary in the theater, where one could pretend without actually kissing.

Whatever the merits of my pathetic attempt at love-making that evening, it must have satisfied Mr. Griffith. I was given the leading role opposite Owen Moore in *The Violin Maker of Cremona*. I shall never forget that moment when Owen Moore put his arms around me. My heart was pounding so fast from embarrassment that I was sure he could hear it.

Making a picture in those days generally took one day indoors and one day outdoors. *The Violin Maker of Cremona* was apparently successful, and Mr. Griffith seemed to be very happy over his latest acquisition. In fact he announced to the heads of the Biograph company that he intended to put me under contract at a guaranteed weekly salary of twenty-five dollars for the first three days, and five for the remaining three. The Biograph people were thunderstruck.

" 'Forty dollars a week for that kid!' " Mr. Griffith told me they shouted. "You're out of your mind." He, in the meantime, had talked me out of the $10 a day with a promise of a guarantee.

In a chorus they demanded to know just what I had that entitled me to ten dollars more a week, on the average, than the others in the company. A very heated argument ensued, and Mr. Griffith told me it ended in his threatening to leave the company unless they agreed to engage me at that figure. Under vehement protest, and with dire predictions of bankruptcy, they agreed.

Following *The Violin Maker of Cremona* I made a film in which I was the mother of several children, the eldest of whom was five years younger than I! I played scrubwomen and secretaries and women of all nationalities. I noticed rather early that Mr. Griffith seemed to favor me in the roles of Mexican and Indian women. Perhaps it was because I was then the only leading girl in Biograph with eyes that photographed dark, though mine are hazel. Whatever the reason, I portrayed them all—Indian maidens and squaws and Mexican señoras and señoritas. I learned to apply thick applications of a red clay mixed with water to my arms and legs with a sponge; often at five-thirty in the cold morning I would don a black horsehair

113

In a 1910 film
"Song of the
Wild Wood Flute"

wig, and a beaded dress weighing many pounds topped by a necklace of alligator teeth.

Even though I was only a child, I gave considerable thought to the problem of acting in those early days. One day I made a vow that I tried never to break. I swore that, whatever the temptation, I would never overact. This was revolutionary in

*Arthur Johnson and I in
"The Little Teacher"
Biograph 1910*

the early movies where the actors were using the elaborate gestures of the French school of pantomime.

"I will not exaggerate, Mr. Griffith," I would say in a firm voice. "I think it's an insult to the audience."

This was only one of many things over which the great director and I squabbled. The argument usually ended with my quitting and being rehired a few hours later.

One day, after our usual squabble followed by an outraged withdrawal to the dressing room, I actually landed in the street, my bag fully and resolutely packed, my mind firmly made up to go home and tell Mother that I was finished with motion pictures forever. I had been playing the part of a misled choir girl in a melodrama called *To Save Her Soul*. At the climax of the story my fiance, played by Arthur Johnson, threatens me with a gun. I had a very hard time reaching the proper

115

pitch of emotion the day we shot that scene. For one thing, Arthur had enjoyed a short nip at lunch and was waving the gun at me as if it were a piece of hose; for another, because of my small stature the back of my long-train velvet dress was held together by safety pins which I had to keep out of the view of the camera. Fuming with impatience, Mr. Griffith strode over, grabbed me by the shoulders, and squeezing as hard as he could, shook me violently.

"I'll show you how to do this thing!" he shouted. "Get some feeling into you, damn it! You're like a piece of wood!"

I reached down and bit him—the first and last time I have bitten anyone—and just as I did so, Lottie, who usually came with me to the studio, sprang on his back, grasped his ears and began pulling on them as if they were the reins of a horse.

With great effort Mr. Griffith shook himself free and stared in wild astonishment at us both.

"How dare you do that to my sister?" Lottie screamed as I rushed to her side.

"Sir," I said, "if I am not an actress you cannot beat it into me. What gave you the right to lay your hands on me? I'm finished with you and motion pictures and the whole thing."

"And I'm finished with you two wildcats!" shouted Mr. Griffith, fondling one ear and then the other as if relieved to find that they were still glued to his head.

Lottie helped me out of the long-train dress. This time I didn't care whether I was rehired or not. I was determined to shake the degrading dust of this studio from my feet and go back to the theater for good. I could do very well, I thought, without these uncouth and loudmouthed motion-picture people. We were on the sidewalk of East Fourteenth Street, turning

116

our steps toward home, shaken but righteous, when Mr. Griffith came running, hatless, out of the building.

"I'm sorry," he said as he caught up with us. "I didn't behave very nicely. You must forgive me. I know you can do that scene. Let's try once more."

The three of us went back to the studio. I was so tense and upset from the violence of our clash that when I was pinned back into my dress, he didn't ever rehearse me.

"Come on, now," he shouted, "let me see the real Pickford! I know you can do it!"

And from all of that emotional turmoil the tears began streaming down my face, the camera ground on, and Mr. Griffith was satisfied.

"A Decree of Destiny"

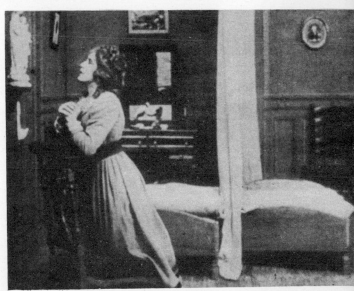

8

As far as I recall, D. W. Griffith never adhered to a script. In most cases, at least in the old Biograph days, I don't think such a luxury had even made its appearance in the studios. Often all he would say to me was, "Mary, you're a scrubwoman," and to Bobby Harron, another Biograph player, "And you, Bobby, are a farmer's son." Improvisation was frequently the order of the day. Sometimes the camera registered an impromptu piece of off-stage action, and that too stayed in the film.

While we were filming a picture called *Wilful Peggy*, taken from *The Country Cousin*, I told Mr. Griffith that I was sick and tired of these wishy-washy heroines.

"I'd like to give this mother of mine in the picture a good shake when she orders me to marry a man old enough to be my grandfather."

"Well, why don't you do it, Pickford?" said Mr. Griffith. "I've no objection."

*With Claire
McDowell in
"Wilful Peggy"
Biograph, 1910*

So poor Kate Bruce, my cinema mother, was grabbed by her cinema daughter and thoroughly shaken. Mr. Griffith eyed the episode approvingly and then went up to Kate.

"What would you do in real life if a sixteen-year-old girl shook you?"

"I'd grab her and spank her good and proper," replied Kate.

"Well, what are you waiting for?" said Mr. Griffith. "Go ahead and do it!"

"If you two think I'm going to submit to this nonsense you're very much mistaken," I said, and I took off and ran around an apple tree, with Kate Bruce chasing after me till she accidently stumbled and fell, whereupon I ran back, sat down, and kissed her, and we put our arms around each other. Both the chase and that little embrace remained in the film.

Kate Bruce, Joe Grable, myself,
Lottie, and Eddie Dillon
in "White Roses" 1910

Jack and I in
"White Roses"

Robert Harron, Kate Bruce,
myself, and Charles Mailes in
"Home Folks"

Another time when my brother Jack and I were acting in the same picture he slapped me harder than I thought the script intended. Bent on revenge, I forgot all about the film and started chasing him, the director at my heels, and the cameraman at his. I finally got hold of Jack, flung him to the ground, and sat on top of him. But he began laughing so hard that I had to join in, and the two of us just rolled over in the dust. The camera, of course, caught every bit of this action and it stayed in the film.

Jack was always the family prankster. If he wanted five cents from Mother he would wait till we were all assembled in a crowded subway car, and begin his routine.

"Mama, give me five cents," he would whisper.

"No," Mother would whisper back; "five cents doesn't grow on trees."

In a louder voice, "Then give me ten cents!"

Mother countered, "I've told you time and again you have to watch your pennies, and the dollars will take care of themselves; and that's just what I'm doing."

Jack's voice rose again. "Mama, I'll talk out loud about your coat."

"Don't you dare!"

Jack, at the top of his lungs: "Put a little Hirsutis on that bald spot in your coat and watch the hair grow back!"

Mother would get terribly embarrassed, and of course Jack got his five cents.

Jack used a similar blackmail on me when I was coming to be known to the growing movie audiences as "The Biograph Girl." In a crowded subway train one day he whispered, "Mary,

122

if you don't promise to give me a dime I'm going to tell everybody in the car that you're The Biograph Girl." The threat sometimes rated fifteen cents, depending on the size of the crowd. It also gave me a peculiar idea of my own which prompted me to ask Mr. Griffith for a ten-dollar raise.

"Are you any better as an actress this week," he replied, "than you were last week?"

I said, "No, sir, but two people recognized me in the subway today. And if I'm going to be embarrassed that way in public, I'll have to have more money."

Mr. Griffith stared at me in frank wonder, then burst out laughing.

"I'll give you just five minutes, Pickford, to think up a better reason than that," he said. "I'd give my whole salary if just one person recognized me in the subway."

It was in a film called *Friends* that I believe the first screen close-up was ever made. Lionel Barrymore and Henry B. Walthall were both in the film, and the close-up was of me. I remember it was late in the afternoon when Griffith shouted to Billy Bitzer, the cameraman:

*With
Henry B. Walthall
and Kate Bruce in
"A Feud in the
Kentucky Hills" 1912*

"Come on, Billy, let's have some fun! Move the camera up and get closer to Mary."

Now that was a startling departure from the then accepted routine of photography. Obediently Billy moved the camera—an unwieldy contraption which weighed about one hundred pounds and in which Billy sometimes kept his lunch. Meanwhile I broke another precedent and put on a second make-up—one a day had so far sufficed for everybody in the business. Billy took the shot, which was a semi-close-up, cutting me at the waist. I was so excited I couldn't wait to see the results. Our projection room was on the second floor, where it had previously served as master bedroom of the old Fourteenth Street mansion. Even more excited than I was Lionel Barrymore, though for another reason. It was in that projection room that, as far as I know, he beheld himself for the first time on the screen. I remember how he stared at his image in frank incredulity.

"Am I really that fat?" he asked me.

I didn't answer, thinking he might let it pass. But he repeated the question insistently, touching my shoulder this time.

"I want you to tell me the truth, little girl," he said gravely. "Am I that fat?"

And I replied, "I'm sorry, Mr. Barrymore, but you are."

"That does it," he said. "No more beer for me."

Mr. Barrymore's excess weight mattered very little to me at that moment. It was the new image of my face that I was waiting to see. What a frightening experience when my grotesquely magnified face finally flashed on the screen! The shock of it was like a physical blow. But I was critical enough to notice the make-up.

"Pickford, what do you think?" said Mr. Griffith.

124

"Friends"

"I think you'll do more of that, Mr. Griffith, maybe even closer."

"You're right, but something's wrong with the make-up. Can you tell me?"

"I think there's too much eyebrow pencil and shadowing around my eyes," I said.

"You're right, Pickford."

When the Biograph heads saw that close-up of me they stormed up to Mr. Griffith in high indignation. Their complaint, as reported to me later, was a classic.

"We're paying this girl the large sum of one hundred dollars a week," they said. "And we want to see all of her, including her feet—not just half of her."

"Pickford," said Mr. Griffith, "it all boils down to this. They want their money's worth."

125

He said he daily bemoaned his fate that he had to be associated with such "dunderheads." He paid no attention to them however, and went right ahead experimenting with new techniques in photography that were soon to make history in *The Birth of a Nation,* and thereafter become the stock in trade of every director concerned with using the camera as a powerful instrument of artistic expression.

9

The following winter, without the slightest fore-
warning, the news broke that the company was
going to take its first trip to California. In those days it took
four night and five days to go from New York to Los Angeles.
When the train was about to pull out, Jack suddenly started to
whimper, "I want to go too!"

"Don't be silly, Johnny!" I said. "You haven't any luggage!"
Mother joined in, "Oh, take the poor little fellow!"
"He's a nuisance, and I don't want him," I said.

The train was already in motion as Mother, undaunted by
my protests, picked my brother up bodily and, with the cry
"Look after your sister, Johnny!" deposited him on the steps
of the moving train.

That flying, last-minute command of Mother's Jack took
very literally indeed. This was January and we were not to return till April, and in all that time he never let a day go by
without dire warning about any man or boy who even looked

at me. To him the most innocent word or gesture, coming from a stranger, spelled irreparable harm to his elder sister.

Our film caravan arrived like a band of hardy pioneers in the thinly populated village of Los Angeles with its eucalyptus palms and heady orange blossoms. Only one other expedition had preceded us into this scattered and undeveloped outpost. That was Broncho Billy's company, Spoor and Anderson, widely known as "Essanay."

Our studio consisted of an acre of ground, fenced in, and a large wooden platform, hung with cotton shades that were pulled on wires overhead. On a windy day our clothes and curtains on the set would flap loudly in the breeze. Studios were all on open lots—roofless and without walls, which explains the origin of the term "on the lot." Dressing rooms being a nonexistent luxury, we donned our costumes every morning at the hotel. Our rehearsal room was improvised from a loft which Mr. Griffith rented in a decrepit old building on Main Street. A kitchen table and three chairs were all there was of furniture. Mr. Griffith occupied one of the chairs, the others being reserved for the elderly members of the cast. The rest of us sat on the floor. Surveying his squatters one day, Mr. Griffith announced he needed a split or half reel.

"Anybody got a story in mind?" he asked.

Three or four of us dashed for paper and pencil and were soon scribbling like mad. During my first weeks at Biograph I had quite unashamedly sold Mr. Griffith an outline of the opera *Thais* for $10. This time I ventured a plot of my own, and to the great annoyance of the men he bought it. It was called *May and December,* and I received a check for fifteen dollars. When Mr. Griffith, shortly after that, rejected a thousand-foot story and a split-reel comedy of mine, Jack and I rented horses and went out to see Mr. Spoor of Essanay. Mr. Spoor gave me a check for forty dollars for the two stories. My greatest competition in this literary sideline was Mack Sennett, who used to claim, teasingly, that my scripts were sold "on the length of my blond curls."

"Let me put your name on my stories," he offered, "and for every one we sell I'll give you five dollars commission on the split reels and eight dollars on the features."

"That's a deal," I said, "but on one condition—I'll have to read and approve of the stories before lending my name to them."

Mack Sennett agreed. A few days later he brought me a story which I heartily disliked. It was overrun with policemen engaged in grossly undignified behavior.

"If you want me to put my name to that story," I said, "you'll have to change all those policemen into private detectives. Their behavior is scandalous!"

He refused indignantly, and that was the end of our collaboration, and the beginning, of course, of the Keystone Cop series.

What with my growing outside earnings Jack and I were soon

In a story I wrote,
"Lena and the Geese"
Biograph 1912

nursing visions of fabulous wealth. My salary remained forty dollars a week, augmented by a liberal stipend of fourteen dollars for expenses. And it wasn't very long before Jack was working six days a week too, at the standard pay of five dollars a day. The poor little fellow had to fall off horses and out of windows as a double for all the young girls in the company. By spring we had accumulated the unbelievable hoard of $1200. I suddenly could not wait to get back East to see Mother and surprise her with our savings.

In April, 1910, Jack and I arrived in New York only to find that Mother and Lottie had not returned yet from an engagement on the road in *Custer's Last Stand.* I promptly went to the cashier of the Biograph company and asked her to change my hoard into twenty-four, new, crisp fifty-dollar bills. Jack and I then bought Mother a handsome black handbag into which we tucked the bills. The moment Mother stepped into the house we presented her with the bag. She was delighted, but it was agony for us to wait till she opened it. Instead of the astonishment we expected when she looked inside all we saw was a pleasant smile.

"Oh, stage money," she said simply.

Mother had never seen a real fifty-dollar bill in her life, and neither had the rest of us. When Jack and I assured her that this was the real business, she counted the bills in a voice of mounting excitement. No sooner had she finished than that rascally brother of mine pounced on them and began throwing them in the air. Mother started chasing Jack around the room, and Lottie and I joined in the pursuit, till we got all the bills away from him. That was the beginning of affluence for the Pickford family.

130

10

There was another reason, I should confess, for my eagerness to get back to New York that spring. I wanted to see Owen Moore again. Actually I had been infatuated with Owen for many months, but I had concealed it that first summer at the Biograph. In Los Angeles I had time to think, which didn't help me one bit. Now I was more smitten than ever.

Owen Moore was five-feet eleven inches tall, extremely handsome, with a ruddy Irish complexion, perfect teeth, dark blue eyes, and a very musical voice. Moreover he was the Beau Brummel of Biograph, always dressed with immaculate elegance. Like the other actors and actresses in the company then, he was using Biograph for what it was worth until he could find a way to get back into legitimate theater.

In the beginning I don't think Owen even noticed me, not in a romantic sense, anyway. Being many years older, he thought, I imagine, I was just a child. If he *was* interested he was more successful in concealing it than I.

Owen Moore

My own feelings were obvious enough for the studio carpenter, Sam Landers, to say to me one day:

"Mary, you don't want to marry an actor. Even if you did, Moore wouldn't be right for you. I hate to tell you this, but I've seen him in the wardrobe sleeping off the effects of a 'beer too many' at Lüchow's."

The story of Owen's drinking wasn't altogether a revelation to me. I had surmised it, but in my helpless state of infatuation it had lost all importance to me.

When I first mentioned Owen to Mother, as casually as possible, her only comment was:

"Owen Moore is too old for you."

The fact is, almost no man would have seemed suitable for me in Mother's eyes. Mother was not only mid-Victorian, she was antediluvian in this respect. I had a taste of her rigorous etiquette some years later when I saw Rudolf Valentino. Mother and I were lunching in a New York restaurant and I noticed a handsome, foreign-looking man sitting opposite us. I was naturally intrigued when he rose and made his way to our table. Very formally and correctly, without so much as a fleeting glance in my direction, he bowed to Mother and said with a marked accent:

"Mrs. Pickford, my name is Rudolf Valentino. I want you to forgive me for taking the liberty of speaking to you without having been introduced. I am very eager to have your advice as to how I may get into motion pictures."

The advice Mother gave him—the first of its sort, I believe —was later to become standard practice.

"Mr. Valentino," she said, "the first thing you must do is to get the very finest photographs of yourself. Spend plenty of

133

money on them. See that there are photographs in profile, full face, bust, and full figure. On the back of each give your age, your height, your complexion, and your experience. Send copies of them to each and every one of the studios. And, above all, have patience."

Valentino thanked her warmly, bowed again, and returned to his table. I must say I was greatly disappointed. Not once had he turned his eyes to me. Mother hadn't given me a single opening.

When he was finally out of earshot I asked her why she had not introduced him to me.

"Why, Mary," she said, "I wasn't introduced myself. And besides I didn't think it was proper in a public place."

Mother probably would have given no more thought to Owen if people in the company hadn't begun to tease her about my infatuation. By then he was a frequent visitor at our home. Finally someone took her aside, told her I was getting much too serious, and that Moore and I were no match.

To my way of thinking Mother now made one of the few big mistakes of her life. She laid down an ultimatum.

"Mary, from this day on you are not to see Owen Moore outside the studio. Moreover, you must tell him that he isn't welcome in our home any more. If you don't I'll have to tell him myself."

Up to then I had been an obedient daughter, but now for the first time I disobeyed Mother. I began seeing Owen secretly. One night I told him, in tears, that we shouldn't be

At seventeen

134

seeing each other so often since it made me very miserable hiding it from Mother. It was then that he proposed.

I didn't know what to say other than that Mother would never permit it.

"Mary," he said vehemently, "if you don't marry me I'll leave the Biograph company and you'll never see me again after tonight."

I was frantic at the thought of losing Owen and frantic at the alternative. In desperation I yielded. A few days later I told the wardrobe mistress at Biograph that I was going to a party and asked her to lend me a long dress with a train. By this time I was wearing high heels every day, not only in my pictures, but on the street. My footing, however, was still none too sure.

After work, dressed in Mother's oversized sealskin coat, the borrowed gown, and high-heeled shoes, I went over to the courthouse in Jersey City and married Owen Moore. If ever there was a sadder wedding I have yet to hear of it. It was on a cold and drizzly January night. Owen and I walked down the misty halls into a dingy, dimly lit room, and as we waited for the magistrate I looked at Owen and a host of thoughts flashed in quick succession across my mind:

"Why, I scarcely know him . . . I don't love him at all . . . What am I doing here? . . . I'm disobeying Mother . . . I don't want to leave my family . . . If I get up and run very fast I may get to the subway before he catches me."

Then I remembered the cumbersome train on my dress, the long flight of stone steps of the courthouse, and my wobbly high heels. Worst of all, I had no money for the subway fare. Had I had more experience I would have real-

136

ized I could take a taxi and pay for it at the other end. Suddenly the train of thought snapped off. I heard my name being called. In a few moments I was married to Owen Moore.

Owen and I returned home, and he said good-by to me at the doorstep. I was soundly asleep in the double bed with my sister Lottie when Mother arrived home, suspecting nothing. Shall I ever forget the following morning? The alarm awoke me at seven, and as I sat up to get ready for work, I looked at my sister's peaceful face on the pillow and at that moment I almost hated her—hated her because she didn't have the terrible burden of guilt that was in my heart. I went to work with my wedding ring hanging on a string around my neck, concealed under my dress. I scarcely spoke to Owen that day.

Now followed several months of bitter self-reproach, of fear, and hiding, and secrecy. I felt guilty of a monstrous betrayal. I never knew when Mother would find out and hadn't the faintest notion what I would say when she did. I lived in the dreadful and growing conviction that I was going to lose Mother and Jack and Lottie, all because I had married Owen Moore. . . .

About that time I broke with Biograph and joined Carl Laemmle's Independent Motion Picture Company (IMP), which later became Universal Films. My new contract with IMP was for $175 a week. A battle royal was then going on between two bitterly opposed camps in the motion-picture industry over the use of the camera. It reached such a bitter pitch at one point that hoodlums were hired to stone the cameras, and even the actors, at IMP. Pending decision of the courts, IMP decided to remove us from the danger areas and ship us to Cuba for three months. Mother, Jack, and Lottie

E*   137 joined me in that expedition, and it was just before we sailed that Owen, who had been most patient till now, insisted that I tell my family about our marriage. Mother cried for three days and nights when I told her, and for the entire voyage Lottie and Jack did not speak to me at all. I still have a vivid picture of Johnny standing at the rail, his cap pulled over his eyes, his arm around his little dog, and tears streaming down his face. I felt like the greatest sinner who had ever lived. What was to have been a long-delayed honeymoon was more like a funeral. Nor was my stay in Cuba any better. I soon discovered that Owen was jealous, not of the other men in the company, but of my family, and my family, of course, returned the compliment with interest.

To make the situation even more intolerable, the director Tom Ince and Owen took an immediate and violent dislike to each other, and Ince's assistant, a man named North, never missed a chance to insult us both. One night North said something rude to me and Owen struck him. North claimed that Owen had kicked him, and called the police with the avowed intention of having Owen put in Morro Castle prison.

It was then that my resourceful mother took over. Before the police arrived Mother gave some quick orders.

"Go to one of the actors you can trust and ask him if he can hide Owen till the police have gone. There's a boat sailing for home tomorrow morning, and we'll put him aboard secretly tonight. And you, Mary, must go with him."

Mother's maneuver worked. When the officers came to take Owen she started a long and heated argument in the course of which two of the men sneaked off with Owen and delivered him safely on board the ship. The next morning, at dawn, I joined Owen on the boat in Havana Harbor, and sailed back to the United States.

As time went on it became more and more obvious what a disastrous mistake my marriage to Owen really was. Besides being jealous of my family Owen deeply resented the fact that I made more money than he did. Luckily he never knew that I always made it part of my contract that he be engaged along with me. I'm not blaming Owen for all the tension and friction in our life together. It was, in many ways, an inadmissible position for any man. I was the leader, and I was so much younger. Those blond curls hanging down my back didn't help matters either. They must have been a grotesque and daily reminder to Owen that a child headed the family.

At the end of my contract with IMP I went for a short while with a company that was formed for me called Majestic Pictures. They agreed at my request to give Owen an opportunity to direct. Again it was carefully kept from him that I had had anything to do with his being engaged. We went to Glen Cove, Long Island, to make the "exteriors." During a scene that Owen was directing I stopped to ask for further instructions. In the presence of my mother and the entire company and crew, Owen lashed out at me:

"Don't put on any of your Mrs. Owen Moore airs around here! Remember you're only Mary Pickford!"

Another black memory was the day I had to undergo an emergency appendectomy in New York. I thought it best not to tell Owen about it, since he was in a very unapproachable mood at the time. As a matter of fact I don't believe he had spoken one word to me in more than a month. I left without saying good-by. Mother alone accompanied me to the hospital.

139

Suddenly Owen burst into my room, berating the doctors and nurses.

"What right," he demanded, "have you to operate on my wife without my consent?"

They tried to reason with him, pleading that my life was at stake, and, because he had been drinking, they had an excuse to do what they did: they gave him a sedative.

Before they gave me the anesthetic I asked them to let me pray for a minute. I did so in silence.

"God," I said, "I want to be obedient; but if it is your wish that I return to Owen I would rather die."

I soon lost consciousness. But the death thought was so firmly implanted in my mind apparently that when I came out of the ether I was saying, "Please, God, let me die, let me die!" And I heard my own voice as if it were coming from someone else.

Since God allowed me to live, I reflected that perhaps it was His wish that I avoid any further unhappiness with Owen.

After the experience in the hospital I wouldn't let Owen come near me. Soon Mother and I left for the Coast. We rented a bungalow in Los Angeles—the first house we shared together since our Toronto days. Before long I was receiving letters and presents of all kinds—from Owen. Then he arrived at the studio himself and begged me to forgive him. And, of course, the usual thing happened: I had a seizure of pity and weakened. I promised to give him another chance.

When Owen moved in with me again Mother wanted to leave, but I wouldn't allow her to. I needed her. I was working fiendishly hard, and, not knowing what lay ahead, I wanted her to be there beside me. Mother was now as eager to make

140

my marriage work as I was, and I remember she got up at five o'clock in the morning, in all kinds of weather, to cook breakfast for Owen, but nothing helped.

While I learned to cope finally with most of Owen's faults —the long fits of silence, the hostility toward Mother, the bitter, masculine resentment of my mounting success—I could not cope with his drinking. One day I faced him resolutely. I was twenty-one and I was now absolutely convinced that there were no happy marriages in the world.

"Owen," I said, "the liquor or I will have to go."

"I'm sorry, Mary," he said "it will have to be you."

That was the climax of what had been five years of despair for me.

I'm grateful that the world is beginning to look upon alcoholism as a disease. Owen may or may not have been able to control his drinking; I shall never know. I do know that he loved me as much as he could love anyone. Perhaps an older woman would have shown greater tolerance. Being a girl, I don't know how I survived the whole dismal experience.

11

During those early years of motion pictures I was billed in theater lobbies as "Blondielocks" and "Goldielocks." In other places I was known as "The Girl With the Curls," though the name that stuck longest was "The Biograph Girl."

My brief sojourn with the IMP company, however, changed matters somewhat. There I was advertised as "Little Mary," so when I returned to Biograph my name, along with the names of others in the company, began to appear on posters and handbills. This was progress indeed, but we were still a long way from having our names on the screen.

I might say here that despite our lack of billing there was enormous rivalry among the girls who vied endlessly and tirelessly for the most prominent parts. I even noticed some resentment when I returned to Biograph, especially among the girls who had stepped up during my absence. There was one part, in particular, that we all wanted to play in a film called

The Sands of Dee. Abundant hair was a requisite of the role. Breathlessly we waited to see who would be awarded the plum.

Mr. Griffith, however, was nobody's fool. While *The Sands of Dee* was still in the offing he began casting for a picture called *Man's Genesis*. As one might easily guess, the heroine of this early epic was expected to wear a primitive grass costume. Mr. Griffith approached me first for the leading role and I refused indignantly.

"I'm sorry, Mr. Griffith," I said, "but the part calls for bare legs and feet." (In those days we even wore stockings and shoes in bathing.)

Blanche Sweet, Dorothy Bernard, and Mabel Normand promptly followed suit. In the end Mr. Griffith announced in a rage that since we considered ourselves above playing this role, he had assigned it to a Miss Mae Marsh, who had just joined the company. With the utmost sarcasm he added:

"And I should like to say for the benefit of those who may be interested that as a reward for her graciousness Miss Marsh will also receive the role of the heroine in *The Sands of Dee*."

Everybody was thunderstruck. Only a short while before Miss Marsh had given up a job at the lining counter of Bullock's Department Store and had come without any previous training in the theater to Biograph.

I still recall how Blanche Sweet's grandmother, who had up to then resented me most cordially, decided to join forces with Mother against the common enemy. Said she:

"Mrs. Pickford, I consider giving that Marsh girl *The Sands of Dee* an insult to our daughters. I don't see how she can possibly play the part. The girl hasn't any hair."

With or without hair play it Mae Marsh did, and of course

144

With Lionel Barrymore in
"The One She Loved" 1911

"An Arcadian Maid"

With Wilfred Lucas in
"Just Like a Woman" 1911

145

we waited for the disaster in store for the company. But a final blow fell: Miss Marsh gave a beautiful performance. Indeed we were all so stirred, we swallowed our pride, and gave her our sincerest congratulations.

The whole episode set me thinking: if a little girl fresh from a department store could give a performance as good or better than any of us who had spent years mastering our technique, then pictures were not for me. I would return to the theater, where the years of study and effort were a safeguard against the encroachment of amateurs.

This resolution was strengthened by the memory of a recent encounter with William de Mille. Mr. de Mille was horrified when I told him about my moving-picture activities—so horrified, I learned much later, that he wrote the following letter to David Belasco:

. . . *Do you remember that little girl, Mary Pickford, who played Betty in* THE WARRENS OF VIRGINIA? *I met her again a few weeks ago and the poor kid is actually thinking of taking up moving pictures seriously. She says she can make a fairly good living at it, but it does seem a shame. After all she can't be more than sixteen or seventeen and I remember what faith you had in her future; that appealing personality of hers would go a long way in the theater, and now she's throwing her whole career in the ash-can and burying herself in a cheap form of amusement which hasn't a single point that I can see to recommend it. There will never be any real money in those galloping tintypes and certainly no one can expect them to develop into anything which could, by the wildest stretch of imagination, be called art.*

I pleaded with her not to waste her professional life and the opportunity the stage gives her to be known to thousands of peo-

ple, but she's rather a stubborn little thing for such a youngster. . . .

In a few weeks now we'll be rehearsing and it will certainly feel good to work with you again in the theater.

Until then, my best to you—

Your friend and pupil
(signed) WILLIAM C. DE MILLE

Mr. Griffith was scarcely sympathetic when I told him of my decision to return to the theater. Laughing scornfully, he said:

"Do you suppose for one moment that any self-respecting theatrical producer will take you now after spending three years in motion pictures? My advice to you, young lady, is to stay where you are."

Stung by the taunt, I replied, "Next year, Mr. Griffith, I shall be back on Broadway with Mr. Belasco."

That was a tall boast; it wasn't so easy for anyone—let alone a Biograph actress—to land an important role with one of the big producers. I still had several months until the theater season started in the fall to prove my boast.

One day that summer a handsome, sweet-faced lady and two pretty young daughters applied at the front office of the Biograph company asking for "Gladys Smith." They were assured there was no one there by that name. When the three of them described some of the pictures I had appeared in, the Biograph man exclaimed, "Oh, you mean Mary Pickford!" And he sent for me.

I came out to greet Lillian and Dorothy Gish and their mother.

"I'll never forget what Mama said the first time we saw you in pictures," said Lillian.

" 'Gladys Smith has fallen from grace. The poor girl must be very poor indeed to have so degraded herself.' "

We were laughing and reminiscing gaily when Mr. Griffith came through the swinging doors into the hall. I beckoned to him and said:

"I want you to meet three of my dearest friends, Mr. Griffith: Mrs. Gish and her daughters Lillian and Dorothy, and I think they would be perfectly lovely on the screen."

"You have courage to introduce me to two such pretty girls," said Mr. Griffith. "Aren't you afraid of losing your job, Mary?"

"No," I said, "because if they can take it from me, it is obviously not my job."

"You'll be sorry," he told me teasingly as he went up the stairs.

One of Mr. Griffith's techniques for bringing us to an emotional pitch in our acting was to make us jealous of each other. Shortly after the Gish girls joined the company he tried this on Lillian and me.

"Pickford," he said to me one day as we started to shoot a scene, "why don't you get a nice costume like Gish's?"

I controlled myself and didn't answer.

"Go upstairs, both of you," he bellowed, "and change your gowns. And don't take all day!"

When we were alone, Lillian and I clung to each other for a few moments.

"I know what he's trying to do, Lillian," I said. "He wants

148

to get me worked up for the coming scene. Lillian, promise me you'll never let him, or anybody else, interfere with our friendship."

Lillian said she never would and she hoped I wasn't angry with her for having a better dress than mine, and that actually, "if the truth must be told, Mary, I prefer your dress to mine."

That evening after supper I couldn't resist being impertinent with His Majesty. I hadn't shown it all that day, but the ungracious allusion to my inferior attire rankled.

"It's too bad, Mr. Griffith," I said, "that you can't get a good performance without trying to come between two friends."

That stung.

"I'll have none of your lip," he snapped. "I'll run my company as I see fit without the insolent criticism of a baby."

"I won't be treated like a baby!"

"Well, that's all you are, and you know it!"

I was a hellcat now.

"Mr. Griffith, I don't care for the way you direct. I never have. If you were a real director you wouldn't have to try to turn me against Lillian to get a good scene. Why don't you think of a more honest way of directing me?"

"I'll have no more back talk from you, you half-pint!"

And with that he gave me a rude shove with his arm and threw me off balance. I tripped and fell. From my position on the floor, on one elbow, in a most melodramatic manner, and conscious of every word and gesture, I scowled at him and said:

"You call yourself a Southern gentleman! You're not only a disgrace to the South. but to the North as well! Never speak to me again, sir! I'm going back to New York!"

149

Mr. Griffith's fury subsided as fast as it had erupted. He was now very remorseful. He made a motion to raise me from the floor, but I waved him away indignantly.

"Don't you dare touch me, sir, or even speak to me again as long as you live!"

I picked myself up and made an elaborate exit to my room. Although I had no serious intention of going home, I had to pretend, after such a dramatic climax, that I was carrying out my threat. I started to pack—noisily.

Mr. Griffith acted even more quickly than I had hoped. He rounded up all the boys and girls in the company, among them the Gish sisters, Bobby Harron, and Jack and Lottie, and the next thing I knew they were all outside my door, serenading me in one voice:

"So long, Mary, how we hate to see you go!"

Of course I melted like a piece of ice in the hot sun, with the result that they all crowded into my room and carried me downstairs to a very contrite and apologetic Mr. Griffith. To celebrate the end of hostilities, Mr. Griffith treated us all to a glass of sarsaparilla.

Episodes like this had their touching and amusing side, but they also made me very eager to keep my boast about getting a job on Broadway. In the early fall I called up William Dean, the manager for David Belasco. To my amazement he had not forgotten me.

"Not Betty . . . little Betty Warren?" he said.

"Yes, Mr. Dean."

"Well, I'll be . . . Where have you been? We've been hunting for you all over."

150

In a shamed voice I told him. "Mr. Dean, I've been in motion pictures."

"So that's where you've been hiding," he said. "Do you still have your curls?"

I assured him I did.

"How long will it take you to get down to the theater?"

"Oh, just a few minutes."

"I can't wait to see the governor's face when he sees his little Betty again."

A few minutes later I was backstage at the Belasco Theatre.

At Mr. Dean's request I took the hairpins out of my hair, removed my high-heeled shoes, and hid myself behind a piece of scenery. Soon I heard footsteps approaching, and I could hear Mr. Dean saying:

"No, Governor, I won't tell you what it is. You'll find the surprise yourself around that piece of scenery."

I was trembling and crying with joy and excitement. The surprise and pleasure on that darling Mr. Belasco's face when he saw me is indelibly imprinted on my mind and heart.

"It isn't true, Bill," were his first words. "It can't be true. Where did you find her?"

"I hate to tell you, Governor, but she's been a naughty little girl. I think we've rescued her in the nick of time."

"And what sort of mischief has my little Betty been up to?"

"The worst possible—she's gone over to the galloping tintypes. But I think we'd better forgive her."

Mr. Belasco then said to me:

"I want you for the part of the blind Juliet, the leading role in *A Good Little Devil*."

I was thrilled beyond words. This was a play written by the

151

wife and son of Edmond Rostand and translated from the original French by Austin Strong.

"Rehearsals are to begin immediately," said Mr. Belasco; "that is, of course, if you are free."

As a matter of fact, I was. I had signed no contract with Biograph, and now my only thought was to dash down and see Mr. Griffith. I broke away just as fast as I could. In no time at all I was bounding up the stairs of the Biograph company. Mr. Griffith was in the midst of rehearsal; I am ashamed to say my taste of triumph overruled my manners. I interrupted, and Mr. Griffith snapped at me. "You know it's a rule that I'm never to be interrupted at rehearsal time."

I was not to be balked. "But this is very important, Mr. Griffith."

"It can wait."

"It can't wait . . . because I start rehearsals Monday for a play and I want to know if it's all right with you. May I go?"

Mr. Griffith's face was a study.

"You're an incorrigible tease," he said. "Please go away! I told you I'm busy."

But he turned and scrutinized my face with such a concerned look that all my triumph vanished in a flash. I suddenly realized how much I would miss my beloved Biograph and the guiding hand of this brilliant man.

Very simply and quietly he said, "Is it true, Mary?"

I handed him the script Mr. Dean had given me. "Yes, Mr. Griffith. Here's the part I'm to play."

"With whom?" he asked.

"David Belasco."

There were tears in his eyes.

152

"God bless you, Mary. I'll miss you very much."

The others had been standing around in silent amazement that one of us, the prodigal children of Broadway, should have been taken back into the sacred fold.

"Mary," Mr. Griffith said as I prepared to leave, "you still have three days to go. Will you report here tomorrow morning? I'd like to make one more picture with you."

Whether it was because it was my last I'm not sure; I do know the picture Mr. Griffith and I worked on for the next three days was the best received of all the films I made for Biograph. It was Anita Loos's *The New York Hat.*

With Lionel Barrymore in "The New York Hat" 1912

The New York hat that caused all the trouble.
The last Biograph film, 1912

The night Mr. Belasco's production *"A Good Little Devil"* opened in Philadelphia, Mr. Griffith and the entire Biograph company occupied the first row of the orchestra.

Mr. Belasco's behavior at rehearsal hadn't changed since *The Warrens of Virginia.* My only wonder was that so far he had somehow overlooked me. I now began to feel I had been spared long enough, that it was only a matter of time. The day finally came when the suspense was too much for me. Wearing the air of a martyr-to-be, I marched up to him and said:

"Mr. Belasco, I can't stand it any longer."

"Can't stand what?" he asked, taken by surprise.

"When are you going to start on me?"

Looking at me in frank amazement, he said, "Why, Betty, what in the world do you mean?"

"Isn't there something I'm doing that you don't like?"

Mr. Belasco gave a friendly and reassuring laugh.

"Don't you suppose I would have told you, if there had been? Now, look here, child," he said suddenly; "I hadn't intended to repeat this to you, because I didn't want to spoil you."

His doctor, a great eye, ear, and nose specialist, had seen our dress rehearsal and commented on my performance.

"Betty," Mr. Belasco said, "that doctor told me you appeared so blind that you must have been living with blind people. He just wouldn't believe you had figured that role out yourself. Feel any better now?"

Naturally the three years I had spent in motion pictures had taught me a great deal about pantomime. But the blindness of

155

the girl Juliet was utterly unlike anything else I had done. It had to be worked out in minute detail. In one act the heroine, Juliet, appears in a garden; in another she is in a house. I would close my eyes and count the steps to the bench, to the door, or wherever I had to walk. When I opened my eyes I would try not to see anything. I can't describe how nerve-wracking it was not to look people in the eyes; to stare blankly over their heads or just beyond their faces. That constant staring was the most exhausting strain of my entire career on stage and screen. When I left for home after the performance I was aching in every nerve, bone, and muscle of my body.

Opening night in New York was one of unprecedented terror for me. I was concerned for one thing about my diction. The dialogue director had cautioned me so much about my Canadian "r's" that I was terrified every time I said the word "garden." Adding to my difficulty was the fact that the cast included veterans of the Broadway stage, like the British Ernest Lawford, all thoroughly seasoned in the subtleties of English vowels and consonants. To my great relief and pride one of the critics complimented me on the very thing that had been haunting me for weeks:

"If Miss Pickford learned her diction on the silent screen, it would seem advisable to recommend that school to the majority of Broadway actors."

For all the physical hardship of the role of Juliet I had every reason to be gratified over my return to the theater. I had promised myself, the night of my first talk with Mr. Belasco, that I would someday have the dressing room then occupied by the leading lady Frances Starr. And now it was mine, a cubbyhole, to be sure, but with the coveted silver star probably costing five cents (before inflation) glued on the door. And Mr. Belasco had the entire room redecorated for me in blue French brocade. My salary was also highly satisfactory. I had truthfully told Mr. Belasco that my pay at Biograph, when I left, was a hundred seventy-five a week, and that was what he paid at the start. Shortly after the opening in New York I told him it would make me very much happier if he could add twenty-five dollars to my weekly earnings.

"My goal, Mr. Belasco, is to earn five hundred dollars a week by the time I am twenty," I announced.

"That's a most excellent reason for you getting an additional twenty-five dollars," he said. "From now on your salary will be two hundred a week."

With Famous Players in 1916

158

12

I said I had every reason to be gratified with my stage work, and yet . . . Almost overnight it came to me: a powerful yearning to be back in motion pictures. I suddenly found myself missing the exciting jigsaw puzzle of a motion picture in progress—the novelty, the adventure, from day to day, into unknown areas of pantomime and photography. I had been so determined never to go back to motion pictures; I had reviewed, almost daily, all the superior attractions of my old home the theater; I had thought of its greater dignity and prouder heritage. But I realized it was useless. I knew I had to go back.

Then one day I read a news story about a man named Adolph Zukor, who had just started a motion-picture company called Famous Players. Mr. Zukor, the paper said, would produce nothing but films of five to six thousand feet, based on the finest plays, and with the outstanding actors and actresses of the world. This was the very thing I had been waiting for. I was fascinated by Mr. Zukor's daring venture and I decided then that I would rather be a small fish in a large pond than a large fish in a small one.

The opportunity came sooner than I expected. Mr. Zukor and his associate, Daniel Frohman, brother of Charles Frohman, bought the rights to make a film of *A Good Little Devil*, with the privilege of using the entire Belasco cast including my understudy—a watchfully waiting little girl named Clare Boothe. It wasn't long after the filming of "The Good Little Devil" that Clare, later to become the famous playwright and ambassador, resigned from the Belasco company. I only learned why many years afterward, when she told me that she and her mother decided that I was much too healthy and that in the normal course of things she would never have a chance to replace me as the blind Juliet. The irony of it is this: I was taken ill the following September and forbidden by my doctor to go on the road. My role went to the girl who took Clare's place as my understudy, a girl called Clare Burke.

In consenting to appear in the film version of *A Good Little Devil* I felt instinctively that a new pathway would open for me, and it did. The picture was a monumental failure. I'm not certain whose idea it was, Mr. Belasco's or the playright's; but we were made to read our entire speeches before the camera. The result was a silent reproduction of the stage play, instead of what it should have been, a restatement of the play in terms of action and pantomime.

The film had taken some four or five weeks to make. My real reward came just as we were finishing it. I was called to Mr. Belasco's office in the Belasco Theatre to meet Daniel Frohman, who with Adolph Zukor had formed Famous Players. I was offered a contract for fourteen weeks at a salary, after

160

much heated negotiation, of five hundred dollars a week. I had reached the goal I had set for my twentieth birthday, and I was just nineteen.

I remained with Mr. Zukor and Famous Players for five and a half years; I have no hestitation in calling them the happiest years of my screen life. I became one of his three children, the others being his own daughter Mildred and his son Eugene; and to the end of our association he was a loving and devoted father.

Every aspect of my private and public life now became Mr. Zukor's watchful concern. I had set notions about what I wanted to do on the screen and off, and so did Mr. Zukor. Sometimes I won, but more often he did. How he worried about me when I was seen in public, and the vehemence of the man on the subject of the clothes I must wear! I never appeared anywhere in the evening without my shoulders swathed in tulle. Even Mother was never more concerned than Mr. Zukor over the people I might be seen with in public. On our way to Boston for an exhibitors' convention, he was horrified when I requested his permission to sit in the club car.

"Mary, darling, are you out of your mind?" he cried. "Didn't you see who just went in there?"

Of course I had . . . and that was why I wanted to go. I had watched her sweep down the red-carpeted platform at Grand Central Station to the special train for the motion-picture people going to Boston for an exhibitors' convention. Sweep down like an empress in her Russian black velvet coat, wide band of red fox about the skirt, enormous red fox muff, matching the tint of her hair, and a huge black velvet picture hat. In awe I had watched her enter the club car, light a cigarette, and, in the presence of all those men, raise a highball to her lips. This apparition was Pearl White, and I was her devoted fan.

"But, Mr. Zukor, I won't stay long," I pleaded.

"The answer is no, Mary honey. Now be a good girl and stay with your Mama and Mrs. Zukor in our drawing room."

When he thought I was deeply immersed in a magazine, he quietly slipped out of the compartment. Just as quietly I tiptoed to the door and peeked out. There was Mr. Zukor blithely sipping a drink and occupying the very seat I had chosen for myself. On Mr. Zukor's face I could see an expression of unabashed rapture as he listened to a story that Pearl White was telling to a small group clustered about her. Once or twice Mr. Zukor would return to announce that he had not changed his mind and that I was not to leave my room.

Along side of this dazzling creature I must have looked like a drab little wren. And I felt like one, that is, till that night, when I linked arms with the Governor of Massachusetts in a great auditorium in Boston. Suddenly, as we toured the arena, great yells came from the crowd: "Hya, Blondielocks! Hya, 'Biograph Girl'!" Meanwhile the Governor was saying, over and over again, as he went along bowing and nodding, "How do you do? Ah, so very nice." Till, abruptly, half stopping in his tracks, he turned to me and said:

"'Blondielocks'? I don't believe I understand. Do you?"

"I do, sir. They are calling me."

"Do they know you, miss?"

"I think they do, sir."

I don't believe that to this day, if he is still alive, the Governor knew exactly what was floating around on his arm.

162

It was the summer of 1914 that I walked into Mr. Zukor's office to ask for my first raise in salary. I still had six months to go on my original contract, which called for five hundred dollars a week, and I had every intention of living up to it. I so explained to Mr. Zukor, adding, however, that I had received an offer of two thousand dollars a week from a rival company on the Coast. Then, as always, it haunted me that every year might be my last in pictures. I never once thought my popularity was anything but a temporary and freakish phenomenon.

"Please know, Mr. Zukor," I said, "whatever you decide to do, I'll go ahead and finish my contract and we'll still be the best of friends."

"I'm sure of that, Mary darling," he said. "Now, let's go and have tea together and we'll discuss it. All right?"

Mr. Zukor took me to a restaurant on Broadway, across the street from a theater where they were showing my latest film, *Hearts Adrift*. After we had sat there some time, Mr. Zukor said:

"Mary, I want you to know that your happiness means everything, not only to me personally, but to my pictures and to my company as a whole."

He paused a moment, then:

"You asked me for more money. How would you like to have your salary doubled?"

I told him that was a very generous offer indeed, and I must have beamed unashamedly at the prospect of one thousand dollars a week.

As we talked over our tea, my eyes would catch the title of the film through the window of the restaurant. I soon began to wonder why Mr. Zukor didn't suggest leaving after we had finished our tea and talk. It began to get dark, and then suddenly I saw it, one of the most thrilling sights of my whole career: my name blazing on the marquee of the Fifth Avenue Theater! That was the first time I saw my name in electric lights. That dear, sweet man had planned his surprise with such loving care, and I had repaid him by asking him for a raise! The respect and thoughtfulness of Mr. Zukor, the patient eagerness to share with me that moment of excitement and accomplishment. Such things endeared Adolph Zukor to me forever.

Despite my concern over money and my fears for the future, I was persuaded to reject a contract with an advertising firm offering me as much as Mr. Zukor was now paying me—$1000 a week, for the commercial use of my name. To make the offer doubly tempting the company also promised an assortment of luxuries that would have vanquished the heart of any girl: dresses by Lady Duff Gordon, the costliest silk lingerie, stocking, shoes, perfumes, cosmetics, fur coats, and even an automobile.

"Mary," said my wise attorney, Dennis F. O'Brien, "I think it would be undignified and risky for you to sign this contract, attractive as it may appear. In time you may find your name being bandied about in all sorts of good, bad, and indifferent commercial projects. You are young; there seems to be a bright future ahead of you. For that future you must sacrifice these articles which are now yours for the asking. Your name should stand for motion pictures and not as an advertisment for evening gowns, cosmetics, and perhaps less alluring products of business." Mother and I were in complete agreement with him. That day I set a pattern in my life and my career which I have followed all my life.

While *Hearts Adrift* was the most successful picture I had made up to that time, it was completely overshadowed by the next one, *Tess of the Storm Country*. Mr. Zukor told me some years later that *Tess* saved him from bankruptcy; that in order to meet the pay roll he had borrowed on his life insurance and pawned his wife's diamond necklace. All I know is that after the release of *Tess* I was Mr. Zukor's fair-haired child.

The entire production of *Tess* in 1914, including my salary and the trip to the West Coast when it was filmed, cost $10,000. One reason we could make a film like this with such a small staff in those days was that everybody was expected to double in brass. Edwin S. Porter, vice-president of Famous Players, for example, was also cameraman, his own cameraman's assistant, director, producer, and head electrician.

The studio, in the back of a dilapidated mansion outside Los Angeles, consisted of a platform with adjustable cotton screens that were run on wires above. The sun did not come over the roof until ten in the morning and it sank behind the back-yard fence at four, which meant that we could not work on "interiors" before or after that six-hour period. Mother and I used all our personal belongings as "props." One of the great drawbacks of the time was that negatives were promptly sent back East to be developed. The result was that we never saw what are commonly called "dailies," that is the work of the day be-

With Harold Lockwood in the 1914 production
of "Tess of the Storm Country"

Second production in 1921

166

fore. Those "dailies" are of immense help in setting the mood of a picture and adhering to it. We were therefore working in the dark. When *Tess of the Storm Country* was completed, it was edited and released without any of us on the Coast having seen a single foot of it. After the long suspense it naturally came as a delightful relief to all of us to learn of its phenomenal success in New York.

In the next few years my salary staged several spectacular leaps, going from one thousand to two thousand; then from two thousand to four thousand, and, finally, to what was then, and, I believe, remained for some time, the ceiling of motion-picture salaries, ten thousand dollars a week. These were not only salaries, but were weekly guarantees against 50 per cent of the profits. These increases did not come voluntarily from Mr. Zukor. From personal observation and study I knew that we had every right to more money than we were at first getting from the exhibitors.

As Mr. Zukor, with much headshaking and ominous prophecy, went on acceding to my demands for higher pay, he raised the price of each film to the exhibitors, bringing the guarantee up from $35,000 to $65,000, then from $65,000 to $120,000, and finally, when he began paying me $10,000 a week, he boosted the fee to $165,000. This, of course, had direct bearing on the type of pictures we subsequently made. We had educated both the exhibitors and the public away from the conception of a five-and ten-cent movie, and sumptuous and spacious movie houses like the New York Strand soon sprang up to prove it.

I might appear to have had a very exalted idea of my own

value in demanding that final jump to $10,000 a week, but my reason grew out of a very practical observation I had made the previous summer. I was driving up Broadway on my way home from the studio one evening when I noticed that a Famous Players picture of mine, *Rags,* was showing at the Strand. As I passed by the theater I saw lines extending from both sides of the box-office. The following week, on the same day at the same hour, I passed the Strand again. Another Famous Players picture was showing there, but it was not mine. No one was standing outside the box-office. Frankly puzzled, I told the chauffeur to turn back and leave me at the Strand. I bought a ticket, went inside, and began a statistical survey. I discovered that the orchestra was less than half-filled. As for the balcony, a cannon could have been fired into it without harming anyone. There was no one there at all. I went home very thoughtful that night. The following morning Mother and I dropped in to see Mr. Zukor.

"How much rental did we receive from the Strand Theater for our picture *Rags?*" we asked.

Mr. Zukor opened his eyes and reluctantly his books and said, "Three thousand dollars."

"And what are you getting as rental for the picture that's showing there this week?"

"Why do you want to know?"

"Well, as we are 50-per-cent partners, we think it's our business to know, Mr. Zukor."

With a sigh of resignation he said:

"Two hundred dollars less, Mary."

I said nothing, but I talked it over with Mother and we decided that when contract time came around again we would

In "Rags,"

insist that my pictures be sold separately, and not packaged with other Famous Players' films.

Mother was always in on my salary and contract talks, and I never knew which one of us he dreaded more. But what else could I do? Other companies were now bidding for my services at staggering figures, and while I wanted to stay with Mr. Zukor, I felt my first allegiance was to my family and myself. Besides I was convinced that the company was well within its means to equal other bids and keep me from going elsewhere. I should add, in fairness to myself, that it was never my intention to hold Mr. Zukor to the agreement in the event that my pictures lost money at the box-office.

170

Famous Players, 1915

It is still incredible to me that every company in the business now began to make fantastic bids for my services. I remember that Universal alone guaranteed me $10,000 a week against 50 per cent of the profits of the combined affiliates. I still wonder whether, after all it wasn't all a dream —a dream from which I never quite woke up. I'm afraid it was more like a nightmare to that sweet and gentle soul, Adolph Zukor, caught between the bidding of rival companies and my legitimate demands for more money.

"Mary sweetheart," he used to say, "I don't have to diet. Every time I talk over a new contract with you and your mother I lose ten pounds."

With Gertrude Norman in "The Foundling"
Famous Players, 1915

With Kenneth Douglas and Glenn Martin
in "Girl of Yesterday" 1915

13

About this time Mr. Zukor was persuaded to merge with the Lasky Company, which included Samuel Goldwyn, Jesse Lasky, and Cecil de Mille. This combination in turn became Paramount Pictures. Where there had been an intimate little family group, threshing out its problems in a warm, personal spirit of teamwork, there was now a huge machine—cold, critical, automatic, and impersonal.

Thanks to the interference from the new parent group I made two pictures, the memory of which I have tried sedulously to wipe from my mind. One was entitled *Less than the Dust*, and I remember how heartily I agreed with a woman who once walked up to me in the street and said, "Oh, Miss Pickford, I loved you in the picture, *Cheaper than the Dirt.*" Because *Less than the Dust* was so incredibly bad, my new masters permitted me to say a few things about the next picture we produced, *Pride of the Clan.* But that was an even more disastrous failure.

To add to the other difficulties, I almost drowned while we were making this picture. We were taking a scene in a small one-cabin fishing boat during the summer of 1916. I was using the cabin as dressing room, when suddenly the director's voice rang out:

"Everybody leave the boat! We're sinking!"

Cast and crew scrambled on both sides, some swimming to shore about three hundred yards away. The women were being lowered into the small lifeboat tethered to the fishing vessel, when I remembered that I had left my cosmetic kit in the cabin. In all that confusion and excitement I started for the cabin, and the odd thing about it is that no one noticed me heading back into the boat. There must have been twenty-five of us. All but Mr. Tourneur were off the boat. Midway to the cabin a voice stopped me. It came from inside of me, the same voice I have heard time and again in my life. I heard it say very clearly, "Don't you go there!"

I rushed back just as Mr. Tourneur was about to step over the edge. We were in water up to our knees. Startled to find me still aboard, he grasped my hand and helped me into the lifeboat. Then he plunged in and swam to safety. But for that mysterious command I would have lost my life. That voice has always been there, guiding me.

I had had another adventure in water—perhaps as close as I ever came to death—in an earlier film I made with the IMP Company. This time it was the Hudson River which was supposed to be the Bosporus for a picture called *In the Sultan's Garden*. Having been caught flirting with an American, I was sewn up in a bag and tossed into the Bosporus from a high tower. Before they stuffed me into the bag, my lady in waiting

174

In "Pride of the Clan" Paramount, 1916

handed me a dagger with which to cut myself free the moment I struck the water. At that point my American admirer, who knew of the Sultan's plans, was to ride in a speedboat to the rescue.

Our camera was on a floating dock. With the cameraman were the director, the rest of the cast, and Mother. I couldn't swim, and nobody seemed to be worried about the dirty water, either. I was told to paddle and tread water as I bobbed up and give the impression that I had cut my way out of the bag.

175

There I was dog-paddling in the water between the camera float and a fast motor launch hired for the scene. In the excitement of being photographed by a movie camera for the first time in his life the captain of the speedboat lost his head. Without my knowing it the speedboat was coming directly at me with what must have looked like an even chance of decapitating me.

One of the men who had been told to keep an eye on me saw the danger and jumped in with all his clothes on. Grabbing my ankles, he pulled me down I would say fully ten feet just as the motor launch shot by overhead and rammed into the floating dock, throwing everybody aboard to the floor.

In the scramble only Mother remembered seeing me disappear. I came up barely conscious and terrified. I can still feel the panic of that moment. I was convinced the man who grabbed my ankles underwater had suddenly gone out of his mind and was trying to drown me!

More and more I came to miss that personal contact with the company that had made it my second family. Mr. Zukor seemed completely bewildered by the new turn of events. Friends, associates, and kin had been talking to him, and he had become a house divided within himself. In that strained atmosphere I now became involved in a rather unsavory issue. Famous Players had promised me a sizable sum before the merger if I would delay signing my next contract.

I went to see Mr. Zukor to remind him of our agreement. In the discussion that ensued I saw Mr. Zukor put his hand under the desk and, I supposed, press a button. An office boy instantly appeared, stating that Mr. Samuel Goldwyn, then Mr.

Goldfish, wished to see Miss Pickford in his private office. Annoyed as I was by this unexpected interference, I went.

"What's all this nonsense?" Mr. Goldwyn flung at me the moment I entered.

"It's not nonsense at all, Mr. Goldfish," I said. "I made an agreement with Mr. Zukor that I scarcely think concerns you. I was put under contract by Famous Players. Mr. Zukor and I will decide it, if you don't mind——"

"Now, you listen to me," he broke in.

"And the next time," I went on, paying no attention, "please don't send the office boy for me. If you wish to see me, come yourself. Good afternoon."

Mutual antipathy started then that is still very much alive today. I wish to say this about Sam Goldwyn, however: he has been at times an inspiring producer; he has artistic integrity; the industry owes much to him because he brought first-rate authors, both of the theater and of literature, to motion pictures. Goldwyn has always had the courage of his convictions. While I do not care to do business with him, I must be frank in my recognition of those qualities of his that have gone toward helping to build the industry.

I am told that Mr. Goldwyn looked out of his office window one day and observed me in the street.

"My God," he is said to have exclaimed. "Ten thousand dollars a week and she's walking to the set yet. She should be running!"

It was while working on *Poor Little Rich Girl* that the advantages of using artificial light from below first dawned on me. I was powdering my nose in the large mirror of the dresser

when a small hand mirror lying at an angle caught the glow of the early morning light and reflected it flatteringly on my face. I went to the studio bursting with my discovery. The moment I arrived I asked my director, Mr. Tourneur, if he would have the cameraman place one of the spotlights down low. Mr. Tourneur laughed at me, enumerating several reasons why it wouldn't work.

"All right," I said. "Let's first take the scene the usual way, and then shoot it the way I suggest. You'll decide for yourself when you see it."

"Just to make you happy," said Mr. Tourneur with a sigh of resignation, "we'll make the experiment."

We did, and the difference was so great that ever since that day they have used the low-lying light to reflect back into the actor's face.

To help with the script of *Poor Little Rich Girl*, I had insisted that Mr. Zukor hire Frances Marion, a brilliant young San Francisco newspaperwoman who was later to write some of my most successful films. Poor Mr. Tourneur—the teasing and wheedling and lashing he had to take from Frances and me while we were filming this picture. We thought we had a masterpiece of comedy on our hands, and where there was not enough comedy we invented little slapstick scenes of our own.

I can see Mr. Tourneur wildly protesting and gesticulating.

"But my dear young ladies, it has nothing to do with the picture. It is not in the play and I do not find it in the script. *Mais non; c'est une horreur!*"

As Gwendolyn in "A Poor Little Rich Girl" 1917

Finally the picture was finished. The day came for it to be shown to Mr. Zukor and the officials of Paramount—one of the blackest days of my life. All the things Frances and I had thought so funny on the set fell absolutely flat in the projection room. I went home to bed without dinner and quietly cried myself to sleep. Frances took it even harder. When she got home she crawled under the bed and wouldn't come out, crying hysterically to her mother:

"Oh, Mother, I want to die! I've ruined Mary's career!"

It was all right for Miss Marion to hide under her bed and want to die. She really had no reason to feel the way she did. But I had to live and face the music. Mr. Zukor sent word that he wanted me to come to his office. It was a meek and chastened Mary who stood before him this time. As gently as possible he told me that I had to be a good girl and not issue so many orders in the future. I nodded and said, "Yes, Mr. Zukor."

Then it came.

"Now, Mary," said Mr. Zukor, "be a darling and go back to your hotel and write Mr. de Mille a nice telegram saying that you were a naughty little girl and that you promise never to do it again."

"Yes, Mr. Zukor. I'm so sorry for everything, Mr. Zukor."

"Now, let me see how fast you can do it, and read it to me on the telephone before you send it. O.K.?"

In the deepest misery I returned to the hotel and wrote what I thought was a most abject note of humility to Cecil de Mille.

"I have no desire to interfere in the choice of stories," read the telegram, "in the casting of the different actors, including myself, and in the final editing. I am placing myself unreserv-

180

edly in your most capable hands. Obediently yours, Mary Pickford."

I did as Mr. Zukor requested, read it to him over the phone, and sent it off to Hollywood. I felt more than ever like crawling under that bed with Frances Marion.

The weeks that followed were one grim ordeal of wretched home life and anxiety about my career. Despite the impossibility of our situation Owen and I were still living together. I had no friends outside the studio; and there was this unending marathon of work, a blessing in many ways, but a deadening weight on my spirit when anything, however small, went wrong. Then came an overwhelming sense of despair and a dismal, lonely, and crucial day at my hotel in January 1917.

I don't recall the incident, but it must have been very upsetting and bitter. Perhaps it was just the last of a series of torments: Owen's constant bickering, and the fact that I had not heard from de Mille, that my whole future, personal and professional, hung in the balance. As I stared out the window of our ninth-floor suite, that snow-covered pavement below suddenly looked very enticing. I caught myself long enough to call Mother, Mother who had stood by in silent torture, yet never once interfering.

"Mama, I need you!" I cried. "You've got to come right now!"

She must have sensed at once what I was thinking, for she spoke very sternly to me, which was rare.

"Don't you dare do anything until I get there. Do you hear me?"

"Yes, Mama."

"I'm getting my hat and coat and leaving right away."

181

The moment she arrived she knew how close we had come to unspeakable horror. Immediately she called the doctor.

"Unless you get this young lady out of here," said the doctor to Mother, "and away from her husband, the least you can expect is a complete nervous breakdown—the very least."

Early the next morning Mother laid the cards on the table to Mr. Zukor.

"Those are the doctor's own words, Mr. Zukor," said Mother, "and that's how things are."

"We'll take her to the Coast, Mrs. Pickford—we'll make a new Mary out of her."

And then Mr. Zukor announced that Mr. de Mille wanted to make some movies with me on the Coast.

The Pickford caravan, consisting of my mother, my sister Lottie, her baby Gwynne, and my brother Jack left New York in January 1917 to take up a temporary residence in California which proved to be permanent.

I had a commitment of two pictures with Cecil B. de Mille, the first, *Romance of the Redwoods*, and the second, *The Little American*, based on the sinking of the *Lusitania*.

I considered it a great honor then, and would now, to work with such an outstanding director and splendid person as Cecil de Mille. His contribution to the development and high standard of motion-picture entertainment cannot be estimated here.

I value highly the friendship that has endured these many years.

At the time I am speaking of, however, I was so frightened of Cecil de Mille I could neither laugh nor cry. I don't remember having a happy moment during the entire filming of *Romance of the Redwoods*. Much of my misery, I'm afraid,

*In Cecil B. de Mille's "Romance
of the Redwoods" 1917*

was caused by the memory of that mortifying telegram. It was
as if I were living in an iron girdle during those weeks. Then
came the surprise of my life. One morning late in March 1917
I awakened to find a deluge of telegrams, twenty-five of them,
all stating, in varying forms of rapture, that our scandalous
misfit, that ugly duckling of a comedy, *Poor Little Rich Girl*,
was a smash success. That was twenty-three more telegrams
than I had previously received after a first showing of one of
my pictures! And the most enthusiastic from Mr. Zukor.

183

With this spectacular turn of affairs I again mounted my high horse, and as Stephen Leacock once said, rode off in all four directions. Once more I demanded to have Frances Marion work with me, and this time Marshall (Mickey) Neilan to direct. Our first picture together was *Rebecca of Sunnybrook Farm*. And that, together with *Poor Little Rich Girl*, gained back the ground I had lost.

In "Rebecca of Sunnybrook Farm" 1917

14

It was on November 8, 1918, the day before the false armistice, that Adolph Zukor and I finally came to a parting of the ways. I was determined to find some way of distributing my films separately from the other motion pictures. My hope was to form an independent company.

"It's a dangerous step, Mary honey," Mr. Zukor said gravely when I first broached the subject to him. "You'll be out on your own, completely and absolutely."

"That's where I want to be, Mr. Zukor."

When another film company, First National, offered me complete independence in the distribution of my pictures, I had one last talk with Mr. Zukor. I decided that if he would equal the bid and grant me similar autonomy over my films I would ignore all the other vexations and remain with him.

"I'll tell you what, Mary," he said. "Think it over while you're having lunch, and then let me know if you still feel the same way."

I agreed. I learned later that, shortly after Mother and I left, one of Mr. Zukor's relatives said to him, "Let her go to First National; I guarantee you it will deflate her swelled head, destroy First National, and bring her back to you on her knees." When Mother and I returned from lunch, it was Mr. Zukor who spoke first.

"I'm sorry, Mary," he said, "I can't meet First National's bid."

"I can't tell you how sorry I am, Mr. Zukor," I told him.

"Call me after you talk to First National, won't you, Mary honey?"

I said I would, and it was like saying good-by forever to a member of my own family.

A few minutes later, on a handshake with J. D. Williams, one of the head men of First National, the new agreement was sealed. I returned to the hotel and made the promised call.

"Mr. Zukor?"

"Yes," came a small, faraway voice.

"I have given my word to First National, and . . ."

There was a long silence; I don't know whether he was crying; I know that finally I had to ask him to forgive me because I couldn't speak.

"God bless you, sweetheart, and I hope you'll be happy."

There was a pause, then:

"Mary honey, now that you're leaving me—I'm going to tell you something—something I always had my heart set on. I'm going to turn my back on the whole star system and build up a chain of theaters across the country."

w York, 1918

187

*"I didn't see
that coal chute!"*

*As Amy Burke
in "The Hoodlum"
First National, 1919*

Which is exactly what he proceeded to do after I broke away from Paramount. He felt that we had grown together, he as a producer and I as a star. In his heart he was almost superstitious. He always remembered it was I who had saved him and his company with *Tess of the Storm Country*. There was more than fatherly affection in this attitude; he was certain that my departure would affect the whole future of Paramount.

Many years later Mr. Zukor and I walked together into the lobby of the huge Paramount Theatre of New York.

"Mary, how do you like your building?" he said.

188

"I don't understand, Mr. Zukor."

"Your pictures made this building possible."

I felt wretched after that telephone conversation with Mr. Zukor. What gain and advantage there might be in the new arrangement seemed trivial and pointless beside the break with a man who had been unfailing friend and father to me. It was victory for me, a false victory in a way . . . not unlike the false armistice that brought the crowds surging into the streets the following day.

From my window at the Hotel Knickerbocker I gazed down on a sea of joyously mad people. All the way up Broadway and across Forty-second Street I could see them. A wave would start eight or ten blocks away and roll like the wind over a wheat field. Society women were seated on top of their limousines, their arms around soldiers and sailors. People were shouting and waving and leaping into the air. Three floors above me a round and beaming face appeared at a window and a voice suddenly burst into glorious song. Presently a second face appeared at a window two floors below, and a second voice, less expansive but deeper in pitch, joined in the most thrilling rendition I have ever heard of the Italian and American anthems. Flags waving briskly from their hands, the celebrants were Enrico Caruso and his Metropolitan colleague and countryman, Antonio Scotti. Ten to fifteen stories above the street, their beautiful tones blended and rose over the noisy carnival below. Mother and I, and perhaps one or two other guests of the hotel, were the only audience of this impromptu concert.

On the day of the real Armistice I was on a train returning to the Coast with the writer Agnes Christine Johnson. During

189

*As Judy Adams
in "Daddy Long Legs*

our four-day trip we mapped out the script of *Daddy Long Legs*
—my next great success. This had been one of two stories that
Mother had earlier gone East to purchase for me. The other was
Pollyanna.

If reincarnation should prove to be true, and I had to come

back as one of my roles, I suppose some avenging fate would return me to earth as Pollyanna—"the glad girl."

While making the film in 1919 I remember I got so sick of Pollyanna in the seventh or eighth week of production that I finally rebelled. I decided the saintly little creature was just too good to be true. There was nothing in the script to indicate the slightest lapse from saintliness in the intolerable weeks ahead. I was appalled at the prospect of unrelieved goodness. My chance to revolt finally came. While the cameras were grinding away one day, I caught a fly on the table, scooped it up and said, "Little fly, do you want to go to heaven?" With that I smacked my two hands together and said, "You have!"

With Mrs. Griffith in "Pollyanna"— first United Artists release, 1920

*My first stand-in
"Maria" 1919, and
the first to be used
in any studio*

That fly in the ointment of Pollyanna's purity was definitely
not in the script, but it remained in the picture. Sickening as
I found *Pollyanna*, the public did not agree with me. It proved
to be one of my most successful pictures. Nor was I ever able
to understand how and why it became a favorite of the
Russians.

It was while we were shooting a scene of *Pollyanna* at the
railroad station in Pasadena that I overheard a child make a
remark I've never forgotten. She was a little girl of about seven,
one of the many spectators who had gathered to watch us take
the scene. "Mama, she's not a real little girl," I heard her say

*In 1919 at the formation
of United Artists Corporation.*

distinctly and astutely; "she's got long fingernails." Needless to say I promptly lopped off the incriminating nails.

Looking like a little girl was quite a problem sometimes—particularly when children were brought into the studio. If I had advance notice of their coming, I would put on one of my little-girl dresses in order not to disappoint them. More often than not I was caught in adult clothes with my curls up on top of my head.

Not long after *Pollyanna* I saw one of my dearest dreams fulfilled—the formation of United Artists. Even with the autonomy offered me at First National I still felt I could create a more efficient distributing service as an independent producer. Then the trade papers reported that the men ruling the industry were planning to clamp the lid down on the salaries of actors. And that was the moment that Douglas Fairbanks, Charlie Chaplin, D. W. Griffith, and I decided to take our leave of the major companies and become our own bosses. When the news leaked out prematurely, someone made the flattering observation:

"The asylum is now in the hands of the maniacs."

With Fairbanks, Chaplin, and Griffith, 1919

15

I have always felt that my meeting with Douglas
Fairbanks was predestined. I had no social life
after working hours. And my only friends were those associated with me in the making of my films. Owen and I, needless
to say, were anything but compatible, although we rarely if
ever went out. One bleak, depressing November day in 1915
we were on our way to Tarrytown, where we had been invited
to visit Elsie Janis at her historic Phillips Manor. . . .

Owen and I sat, gloomy and silent, in the back of a conservative black limousine. Some miles out of Tarrytown we
passed a low-slung foreign car with a half top, and I noticed
that the couple sitting in the back had a leopard rug over their
laps. I wasn't quite sure that I approved of this showy car or
that flamboyant lap robe. Our chauffeur wasn't certain of
the way, so Owen had him stop the car at the next crossroad,
which, as it turned out, was also a crossroad of my life. As
Owen got out to look at the sign the low-slung foreign car drew

up alongside and a very agile young man jumped down and joined Owen. I saw them beam in recognition and shake hands. The two of them strode over to our car and Owen said:

"I want you to meet Douglas Fairbanks. . . . This is my wife Mary."

I didn't meet Mrs. Fairbanks until we arrived at Phillips Manor.

I had seen Douglas twice before, the first time when he appeared on Broadway in a play entitled *A Gentleman of Leisure*; the second time in his first motion picture, *Bertie the Lamb*, which he had previously done in the theater. With that film he attained full and immediate stardom with the Triangle Company, and was now receiving the largest salary per picture in the whole industry.

Elsie Janis and her mother had legions of friends among the artists, and many of them were at Phillips Manor on that dismal November day when our limousine drew into the driveway. I exchanged greetings with a great number of people, and, suddenly feeling very depressed, I retired into a corner with a fashion magazine. Every now and then my eyes wandered to a laughing huddle in the center of the large reception room, and I found myself disapproving heartily of the exuberant Mr. Fairbanks. Nor did Elsie make me any happier, playfully flirting with every man in sight. Suddenly I saw her dashing down the stairs shouting:

"Come on, Doug! Come on Owen! Let's all three of us go for a walk." Then, looking at Mrs. Fairbanks and me, "You girls don't mind if I steal your husbands for a few minutes."

Owen and Douglas trooped off with her like a couple of mischievous schoolboys.

"Come on," I said to Mrs. Fairbanks, "let's go for a walk too. We're not going to let her get away with that."

Elsie, Owen, and Douglas were already some distance ahead, when Mrs. Fairbanks and I followed. A few moments later I saw the three figures disappear over a hill and down an incline.

"Let's hurry after them," I said.

But Mrs. Fairbanks protested that it was too cold and that she was going back to the house. I went on alone and caught up with them at a stream which they had just crossed. A log lay across the icy water, and as I cautiously set one foot on it, Elsie shouted from the opposite bank:

"You'll ruin those beautiful new shoes of yours!"

And I shouted back, "What's a pair of shoes to losing a husband?"

I was wearing a tight-skirted Russian-style dress of black velvet, with a white satin blouse, Russian boots, half patent leather and half white kid, all very beautiful and all brand new. Thus clad, I proceeded to navigate the log. The three fugitives had meanwhile disappeared around the bend.

After taking a few timid steps I stopped, midstream, immobile with fright. I knew I couldn't possibly negotiate it without falling into the icy water. What followed was typical of Douglas. At the precise moment of my sudden panic he decided to turn back. What a relief it was to see his friendly face smiling at me.

"Do you mind?" he said.

And I frankly replied, "No," when I saw how he planned to rescue me. "Please do."

He swept me up into his arms and leaped back to the other side, where we were joined by Elsie and Owen.

I didn't think of the episode in a romantic light—at least not at the time—and I'm quite certain Douglas didn't either. It was a gesture he would have made to any woman in such a predicament. I don't recall giving him much thought after that meeting. I buried myself in my work, and in fact tried to do as little thinking as possible, about myself. I hadn't the remotest suspicion that I would or could ever fall in love, again. Moreover I was convinced that a happy marriage was a schoolgirl illusion. I was resolved to take my marital punishment with a grin. I had carved out my future in my career. It was my solace, my high fortress, where no one and nothing could molest or harm me. So I thought and so I strove to make it.

Then I met Douglas for the second time. I was living at the Knickerbocker Hotel, in New York, and he at the Algonquin. Frank Case, the proprietor of the Algonquin and a very close friend of Douglas (later to become, with Mrs. Case, beloved friends of mine, too), gave a dance to which I was invited. Since it was Saturday night, I again did the unusual thing of accepting. Between dances Douglas and I sat on a couch in the hotel lobby and talked about motion pictures.

"Do you know who are the two outstanding artists in pantomime?" he asked me, and amazed me by naming Charlie Chaplin and myself. He went on to say that I had mastered the art through a great economy of gesture.

"You do less apparent acting than anyone else I know, and because of that you express more," he said in that warm, emphatic way of his.

I thought at first that he was joking and told him so. I was unaccustomed to being spoken to that way. Owen was more likely to belittle my work than to praise it. It was like a breath of new life listening to Douglas' praise. I hugged the echo of his words for days, repeating them over and over again to myself. . . . I had been living in half shadows, and now a brilliant light was suddenly cast upon me, the sunlight of Douglas' approval and admiration.

How can I possibly convey the impact of this man's personality, the terrific vitality, the completely childlike enthusiasm? One would have had to know Douglas personally to realize the overwhelming dynamism of the man. People of attainment fascinated him, and he them. He sought them out, not because he was a snob, but because of his lively interest in how they had made their names; how they accepted their successes; how it had influenced them. I don't think either of us realized, after that second encounter, that we were falling in love. When the realization came, it was too late to save the loneliness and heartache and escape the cruel spotlight of publicity. We fought it, we ran away from it, not once, but times innumerable. Mother knew, and so did Douglas' mother, and she was always tender and loving to me.

Whenever I avoided going anywhere I knew Douglas would be, I consoled myself by calling his mother on the telephone or visiting her the next day. The sound of her voice, or the look on her face, which so vividly reminded me of him, would somehow ease the pain.

Douglas' mother was a gay and charming little lady from Virginia, a descendant of the Earl of Nottingham. Douglas was her pet, and to the end a wonderful son. Her death came as a cruel and sudden blow to him. She contracted pneumonia at Christmas time in 1916, while he was in California, and passed away before he could get back to New York. When he arrived

I heard that he was unable to cry and all his friends were concerned about him. I wrote him a short note of comfort. The following day he telephoned me and asked if he could see me for a few moments.

For one hour we rode in Central Park in my chauffeur-driven car. This was a day or so after his mother's funeral. For the first time he was able to talk freely about her, and what she had meant to him. The emotional storm that had gathered in his breast finally burst, and he was able to cry. We never spoke of ourselves, only of his mother, and her death seemed to bring us closer. Douglas went back to California, and I remained in New York. Later, when he returned to New York, to stay with his family, I went to Hollywood, and was with the Paramount studio when he joined that company in the spring of 1917. Although I saw him in the studio from time to time, we still fought the inevitable. In the meantime I had separated from Owen and was living with my mother, my brother Jack, sister Lottie, and her baby Gwynne.

Neither Douglas nor anyone else separated me from Owen. He did that himself. Naturally a great attraction like that between Douglas and me could not remain concealed forever. Owen came to me one day, stating he had the right to know since he was still my husband—although we had ceased to be man and wife. I told him the truth, and he asked what I was going to do about it. I replied, frankly, that I wasn't planning to do anything.

It was in the fall of 1918 that Beth Fairbanks and Douglas decided to part, and soon they were divorced, and shortly thereafter Mrs. Fairbanks remarried. Beth and I always had

200

the greatest respect for each other. There was never any ill-will between us, and neither was there between her and Douglas.

Much as I loved and needed Douglas, for almost a year after his divorce, I still fought the thought of a divorce of my own. Divorce seemed to me then as it does now a form of amputation, to be avoided even at the cost of my own happiness and that of the man who loved me. It was a black and indecisive period for me. Although separated from Owen, I still felt his possessive presence in one form or another. Then came a final meeting with him that is etched on my mind with letters of fire. He asked for a reconciliation.

"I'll even be nice to your mother if you take me back, Mary."

"My mother does not need you or anyone to be nice to her, not as long as I live; and besides, you're several years too late for that speech, Owen."

I'm sure the impeccably groomed Mr. Moore was oblivious of the tears that were streaming down his face, meeting in a rivulet under his chin, and dripping down on his immaculate tie; oblivious of all this when I told him that I was finished.

"Owen, I want a divorce."

Now he grew ugly.

"Mary, so help me, the next time I run into Douglas Fairbanks, I'm going to shoot him dead!"

"You're going to do nothing of the sort, Owen," I said calmly, though frankly I was terrified because if Owen were drinking he certainly could not be responsible for what he might do. I appealed to his sense of fair play.

"Owen, why should *you* resent him, *you* who, not once, but a hundred times, have thrown me aside."

G*

"I won't have it, Mary! Mark my words, I'm going to kill that climbing monkey! I just won't have it! You understand?"

I immediately called Douglas to warn him about Owen's threat. Douglas laughed it off.

"I can take care of myself, Mary darling," he said. "Don't you worry your dear little head over it. I'd sure like an opportunity to get at him for what he's done to you all these years."

I learned that Owen was actually carrying a gun in public and openly threatening to shoot "that climbing monkey" on sight. Douglas, however, never tried to avoid him. There wasn't a bit of cowardice in his make-up. Then came the bombshell —the final and most bitter humiliation of all. Through his attorneys Owen informed me that he was ready to grant me the divorce—for a price.

If any spark of tenderness or compassion remained in me, that last act of cold calculation killed it. I was so thoroughly disillusioned that I knew, as I had never known before, that any solution short of divorce would be a cruel and needless torture. I must wipe out the tragic blunder that was blighting my life and my career once and for all. I consulted Mother. Agreeing that there was no alternative, she went to our bank in Los Angeles and was coming out with a fat bundle of bonds under her arm, when, of all people, she ran into Owen's mother. I believe Mother told her what was in the bundle, for Mrs. Moore then made the only remark she was ever heard to make that might even slightly indicate any hostility toward me.

"Oh, sure, Mrs. Pickford, poor Owen must have something."

They were both highly embarrassed, Mrs. Moore probably more than Mother, and I suppose she meant, with the motherly love she bore both of us, that her son should in some way be compensated for having lost me.

A period of severe tension and anxiety now followed. I was haunted by having had to pay for my freedom in hard-earned money; by the growing danger that the newspapers might get wind of the unsavory transaction; by the certainty that people would be saying that I had bought off one husband to acquire another. And looming ahead of this whole dismal scene was my divorce. A year earlier Mother had gone to Tahoe to place a deposit on a house that had caught her fancy on the Nevada side. I then had every intention of spending a part of each year on vacation there, and already considered myself a resident of Nevada. But to qualify for a divorce in those days one had to live six months in the state. Mother, my beloved attorney Dennis F. O'Brien, and I went to live on a farm in a town called Genoa, not far from Minden. No one can blame the farmer and his wife for assuming it was either Mother or Mr. O'Brien who was getting the divorce. They never even suspected that this little creature with the flat-heeled shoes and blond curls falling down her back was married. Despite all our caution a horde of reporters finally got wind of my being in Nevada. A great newspaper dragnet was set out for me. Mr. O'Brien and Mother decided we had to move quickly. After three weeks in hiding on the farm we slipped into Minden. I never in my life felt so much like a hunted animal. When I finally got my divorce the first of March, 1920, I promised myself that I would wait one whole year before marrying Douglas. With complete sincerity I informed the press, when it caught up with me, that I had no immediate intention of remarrying. Unfortunately I was reckoning without Douglas, a persuasive and relentless advocate when he had made up his mind. He argued and pleaded and cajoled. Arrayed against him was every force, individual and collective, in Hollywood. We were warned that our pictures might become total failures at the box office, that our hard-won prestige would be buried under an avalanche of malignant gossip and denunciation. Whether we wanted it or not, the roles we portrayed on the screen had built up a special picture of Douglas and me in the world's eyes. Both of us, I perhaps more acutely than Douglas, felt this obligation to the public. It was a step that neither of us could take lightly, or did.

When I asked Mother to guide me through this crisis, she said simply that it was time that I had some personal happiness in my life. My brother and sister also encouraged me to marry, although the possible consequences meant a great deal to their future too.

When I finally yielded, I did so because I loved Douglas. After all the suffering and falseness of my first marriage I wanted to be true to myself. I still remember the last talk we had before I consented to marry Douglas.

"Mary," he said, "the world doesn't know the true facts of our love and the suffering we went through to find one another. If it did know, I am confident it would approve of our marriage."

"What if the world doesn't approve," I said, "will your love be strong enough? If we both lose our careers, will our love be sufficient for our future happiness together?"

"I can't speak for you, Mary," he said, "but I know that my feeling for you is not of the moment. It has nothing to do with your career or your fame, or how other people feel about you. I love you for yourself."

On March 28 Douglas and I were married quietly in Los Angeles by our good friend the Rev. Dr. Whitcome Brougher in his home. Apart from one or two very close friends only members of our immediate families were present, Mother, Douglas' elder brother Jack, and his wife. For the wedding supper we returned to Douglas' home in Beverly Hills, the beautiful house that was to become my permanent home, and soon to be named by the press "Pickfair." Douglas had been living there alone for a year.

"Mary," he said when we arrived, "this house is my wedding present to you."

"No, Douglas," I said. "I want to feel that this is your home, and that I am sharing it with you."

Our marriage remained a secret for three days. I was making a picture called *Suds* at the time, and for those three days I came into the studio with a piece of adhesive tape over my wedding ring, which I was very superstitious about removing. I learned later that, clever as I thought myself, I fooled no one in the company. Then the bombshell burst. First the straight news of our marriage in massive headlines everywhere; then a review, mostly speculative, of the long romance that had preceded it; and finally the nasty repercussions of my divorce. . . .

Of course today people don't think anything of going immediately from the divorce court to the chapel. In those days divorce seemed to most of us like some dreadful disease.

Reporters and columnists and photographers began hounding me about the legality and duration of my Nevada residence. They chose to forget, or never knew, that I had intended to

make my permanent residence in the state of Nevada and to wait a full year before considering remarriage. They said I had sworn falsely in stating that I had intended to spend part of every year in Tahoe. My sincerity and veracity were challenged in lurid headlines. Most cowardly and disgusting of all was the statement that a baby was on the way:

"What will its name be," the newspaper asked, "if the State of Nevada invalidates the decree on the grounds of inadequate period of residence? Will its name be Moore, Fairbanks or Pickford?"

To advertise a syndicated article, they pasted a big picture of me on the news wagons. The photograph was greatly enlarged and huge glistening tears had been sketched in on the face. That coy little touch was meant to convey my shame and penitence over the great wrong I had done. But Douglas and I were soon to forget these irritations in the overwhelming show of popular affection that greeted us everywhere we went in Europe. For the moment I finished the picture *Suds*, Douglas and I left for a four-week honeymoon abroad. After the marriage neither of us had any suspicion of what lay ahead for us either in Europe or in America, on our return. This was by no means a publicity safari or experiment, however. I had never seen Europe. In fact, except for that one brief sojourn in Cuba, I had never been out of the United States and Canada. Douglas, who was an expert traveler, prepared the way. New York gave us a heart-warming reassurance that all was not lost. So dense were the crowds that we didn't dare to set foot out of our suite at the Ritz-Carlton Hotel.

The dress I wore when I was married to Douglas

On our honeymoon

Then the trip to Europe. On board the boat we were drawn into a friendly circle of well-wishers and admirers that included Colonel House, Ambassador Gerard, the widow of O. Henry, Sir William Wiseman, and a big financier whose name now eludes me. Between chats and discussion and walks on deck, Douglas and I studied Dickens' *A Child's History of England.* I remember it excited me to such a degree that I couldn't sleep. I was convinced that once I set foot on English soil I would instinctively, even blindfoldedly, be drawn to places that seemed to rise up in memory from my ancestral past.

Instead Douglas and I were swept up by mobs of fans till I could neither eat nor sleep, let alone drink in the historic sights. Our first stop was the Ritz in London. Outside our window we saw them, thousands and thousands of them, waiting day and night in the streets below, for a glimpse of us. I felt so inadequate and powerless to show my gratitude that it actually made me ill. How I longed then to be a Jenny Lind and sing to them my heartfelt appreciation! Of course this was 1920. We had just come through a frightful war. Hysteria was still in the air, a fevered tenseness from the accumulated war fatigue, and a pent-up delirium that could go off at the slightest touch.

Then there were the newspapers and photographers. It's no wonder that when Lord and Lady Northcliffe visited us at the hotel, they found me shaking like a leaf.

"Why, this young lady is on the verge of a breakdown," said Lord Northcliffe to Douglas.

"She hasn't slept or eaten anything since we arrived," he replied.

"I have been receiving all sorts of patented remedies and even home-baked breads," I said. "Word must have got around that we are being held incommunicado and starved by the authorities."

"There's only one thing for you to do," said Lord Northcliffe. "I insist that you go to my country place on the Isle of Wight. There you may enjoy complete seclusion. The rest and peace will do you both good. I promise absolute isolation."

So it was off to the Isle of Wight for Douglas and me. And there, at six-thirty the next morning, I awakened, went to the window in my nightgown, threw open the shutters, and gasped. The ten-foot brick wall surrounding the cottage was black with people. From dawn they had been waiting patiently on the top of that wall for those shutters to open. And now they all proceeded to applaud loudly and call our names. Douglas awoke with a jolt and ran to the window to see what was going on. Then we both dashed back into the room and slipped

209

hurriedly into our dressing gowns. Meanwhile the crowd began crying out:

"Oh, Mary darling! Come out."

"How are you, Dougie?"

"Won't you come out and give us your autographs?"

I was still giving my hair a few quick strokes of the brush as Douglas returned to the window and began waving to them. When they insisted on a speech, he spoke a few words of greeting, and when I joined him I did the same.

"This is such an overwhelming surprise that I wish there were some way we could repay you," I said.

They were most considerate. After a few more shouts of "Hello, sweetheart!" "Hello, Dougie!" they went away quietly. Douglas and I breathed a sigh of relief and proceeded to dress.

"Absolute isolation!" he said.

And we both burst out laughing. More of the "rest and peace" of the Isle of Wight were to be ours that afternoon when we went out for tea. The crowds were even thicker this time. They pressed in very close and Douglas and I were soon aware that a frantic and uninhibited souvenir hunt was on. When we took inventory later in the day, Douglas had lost all the buttons off his coat and vest, and I had surrendered my handbag, powder case, and handkerchief. Even the hairpins in my curls were gone. It was a most flattering if utterly bewildering thought that here on the Isle of Wight, so far away from California, people actually knew and loved us as if they were our neighbors in Beverly Hills. I adored the English, and, having been born in Canada under the Union Jack, I felt completely at home with them. But I found this same warmth and friendliness everywhere: Paris, Rome, Alexandria, Moscow, Tokyo . . .

210

We of the silent screen enjoyed a unique privilege. Through our voiceless images we were citizens of every country in the world. This world citizenship of the screen we threw away with the advent of talk.

Back in London from our "seclusion" on the Isle of Wight, we were given a large luncheon and reception at Claridge's Hotel by George Grossmith and other distinguished British actors. Douglas sat on one side of me and Grossmith on the other. During the luncheon Douglas leaned across me and said:

"George, have you arranged for police protection for Mary?"

"My dear chap," Grossmith replied, "you don't seem to realize that you're in England now. The English are a civilized people. They're not going to harm Mary. Depend on it."

I was to learn the folly of his words in Kensington Gardens that afternoon. A brilliant outdoor benefit, a sort of garden party and bazaar combined, was scheduled, and all the professional people were expected to appear. Grossmith and his colleagues of the stage invited us as their guests. Word of our coming must have spread like fire. Grossmith, Douglas, and I were seated in the back of an open Rolls-Royce. I remember the car had slowed down as we moved into the park grounds. On all sides the crowds were thick as bushes, waving and shouting wildly. Suddenly a voice called out, "Shake hands with me, Mary!"

While my two companions were looking the other way I put out my hand. Immediately I felt it lock in an iron grasp. Then someone else grabbed my other hand, and two or three people reached for the rest of me. I was quietly but surely sliding over the back of the moving car, when Douglas turned his head and quickly lunged out for my ankles. The car stopped, and as

In Kensington Gardens, 1920

Douglas held on, a frightened and bewildered Grossmith began gesticulating wildly.

"I say, please unhand the little lady, won't you?" he spluttered. "Can't you see she's in danger of her life?"

Finally the crowd let go of me and I slumped into the back seat of the car and caught my breath. That was only a brief rest between rounds, however. When we got out of the car, the crowds closed in like quicksand, and for the first time I found myself perched on Douglas' shoulders.

With this immovable mass around us we started for our goal. We were making progress when the low branch of a tree suddenly barred my way. In all that excitement Douglas at first didn't realize what was happening. When he saw the branch across my chest, he quickly kneeled to clear me. In doing so he almost lost his footing, and both of us were catapulted into a tent, where two elderly dignified English ladies were standing guard over a large array of homemade jams and preserves.

The ladies stared at us in great astonishment and tried to be hospitable and polite. But their attitude changed swiftly as the crowd pressed forward and stormed the little tent, knocking all the neatly assembled pots and jam jars to the ground. In no time at all we were all walking around in a sticky goo that seemed inches deep, till the two staid and elderly ladies finally lost their tempers and drove us out of the place.

Douglas and Grossmith half carried me to a small English car that someone had commandeered. The car was parked on a nearby footpath. Along the path, on both sides, were countless park benches bulging with men, women, and children. As Douglas and I were bustled into the car, I looked out the back window and had my last glimpse of the usually impeccably attired George Grossmith standing in the middle of the footpath, silk hat missing, carefully groomed hair standing on end, tie awry, collar flying in the wind. Very plainly and unabashedly he was waving us away, glad to see the last of us.

In somewhat less hectic circumstances we finally rounded out our week in England and crossed over to Holland.

In Amsterdam we were met by the city's top officialdom, many of them loaded with presents. The crowds were very much like the crowds of England, on a slightly smaller scale, perhaps, but fully as demonstrative. The same barrages of questions from newspapermen; the same batteries of cameras. It was nothing in those days to count forty reporters in the room. Answering so many questions at once—most of them in translation—was a trying and risky business. In Holland, Douglas decided I needed a real rest in a place where our names meant nothing to the crowds. The answer, of course, was Germany. Several years had gone by since our last pictures were shown in that country. If our names were known there at all, it would almost certainly be with hostility, because of anti-German speeches and propaganda films Douglas and I had made in the Liberty Bond drives.

"Hipper," Douglas said, using his favorite nickname for me, "we won't be liked in Germany but at least we'll be left alone."

Douglas rented a car and we started on our journey into what had so recently been enemy territory. The Dutch stopped us at the border and we had to take a streetcar into Cologne. Poor little undernourished German schoolchildren stared at us in open resentment, realizing, I suppose, that we were wellfed foreigners.

214

Going into the magnificent cathedral of Cologne, where English occupation troops were now quartered, I thought how strange it was to see erstwhile enemies, both English and German, many of them with black mourning bands on their left arms, kneeling together in common prayer to Almighty God. I couldn't help wondering what the Supreme Being thought of us benighted mortals at that moment.

Douglas and I proceeded down the Rhine to Wiesbaden, where the French were in occupation. In Cologne we had been told that a great number of English boys had married German girls and were already proud papas of blond little Teutons. Not so the French. There was no fraternizing that we could see in Wiesbaden; no kneeling together; no intermarriage. The French soldiers remained coldly aloof, with dour expressions and tightened lips.

It was in Wiesbaden that Douglas and I changed our minds about one thing: no matter how demanding and exhausting the crowds were, they were infinitely preferable to being either completely unknown, or, if known, completely ignored. After a day of shopping and sight-seeing, during which we did not catch a single flash of recognition on anyone's face, Douglas asked me:

"Frankly, Mary, how do you feel about it? Do you like being left alone?"

And I said, "I definitely do not, Douglas. Let's go some place where we are known. I've had enough obscurity for a lifetime."

I'm afraid we were already becoming spoiled. So we moved farther down the Rhine to Coblenz, which was occupied by American troops. The general commandeered quarters for us in a lovely German house, and we spent the Fourth of July there looking over the Rhine at the beautiful Castle Ehrenbreitstein on the opposite bank. From our vantage point we could watch the brilliant display of fireworks. First a huge American flag blazed in a thousand lights and then a massive picture of Woodrow Wilson flashed on the night sky and went rising up to a lingering fade-out.

Of course I had to mar that exciting and memorable day by dancing with the general in command. . . . To explain the nature of my misdemeanor, I must go back a little. The night of our wedding Douglas had gravely said to me:

"I'm your husband now, Mary, and I don't expect any 'two-sing' with anyone but me at dinner tables, in theaters, or on dance floors. Have I your word?"

Just as gravely I said, "You have, Douglas!"

I knew Douglas was a jealous man, but how fanatic he could be I never suspected till that Fourth of July in Coblenz.

The commanding general paid me the honor of asking me for the first dance. I hesitated a moment, too embarrassed to explain that I had promised not to dance with anybody but my husband. Then I accepted the general's invitation.

Douglas maintained a good front for the rest of the evening, but he was boiling. All the way back to our quarters he didn't say a single word to me. I could feel the anger seething inside him, ready to erupt at any moment. When we got to the door of the house where we were staying, he abruptly turned on his heels and vanished down the dark street. There I was alone in a German house, wondering when Douglas would cool off and return, and if he would return at all.

A childish fear began to close in on me: I remembered all

216

the rabid speeches I had made against Germany and the Kaiser during the Liberty Loan campaigns. I was certain the news of my belligerent behavior had reached the people of Coblenz and that they were secretly waiting for an opportunity to avenge themselves. I could feel my throat being very quietly slit in the night. I was afraid to lock the door, because Douglas might come back at any moment, and I might be asleep and he wouldn't be able to get in; that he might suspect I was punishing him for his boyish peeve, that he might begin battering down the door and bringing the whole American Army of Occupation to the scene.

It seemed an eternity before I heard the sound of footsteps; yet only one hour had passed.

"I'm sorry, Mary," he said. "My behavior was uncalled for."

I told Douglas then that I would never break my promise again, and no matter how mortifying the circumstances were, I kept my pledge.

Many years later we found ourselves in a night club with a small group of English friends, among them Prince George— later the Duke of Kent. The Prince asked me to dance, and this time without a moment's hesitation I refused. I saw the puzzled look on his face.

"I'm deeply sorry," I said, "but the truth is I do not dance with anyone but my husband. I'm most embarrassed to refuse so great an honor. But it is a promise I made to Douglas."

As I heard my outer voice make this prim little speech to Prince George, my inner voice was saying, "How pompous and self-important that sounds." If the ground under my feet had only opened and swallowed me, I would happily have pulled the hole in after me.

217

The Prince could not have been more gracious and considerate.

"My dear Mrs. Fairbanks," he said, "I quite understand. I think one should observe the rules of the game, whatever the game may be. I would be sorry indeed to have you break your word for the selfish pleasure of dancing with you."

Douglas and I were always seated beside each other at dinner, wherever it might be and whoever else was there. Sometimes it was painfully difficult for me to explain to the host and hostess in advance. Often very careful arrangements to seat us apart would have to be modified on short notice. My explanation usually went as follows:

"Douglas and I have made it a rule to sit together always, both at home and elsewhere. I trust it won't inconvenience or upset your plans for the seating of the table. If you can possibly arrange it, I would appreciate it. . . ."

Our hostesses were usually too well bred to make any comment, at least not in my presence, other than to assure me that they quite understood. I wonder if they did; indeed I often wonder if I understood this idiosyncrasy of Douglas myself.

From Germany, Douglas and I moved on to Italy. Again we were enthusiastically received and it was from the mouth of an Italian boy that Douglas heard himself called "Lampo" ("Lightning") for the first time, a name that stuck wherever Italians gathered to watch his films. As we pulled into Lugano at seven o'clock in the morning, this little boy saw us and went dashing down the street, screaming in a high and excited voice, *"Maria e Lamp—artisti del cinema!"* In a matter of minutes what seemed like the whole populace of Lugano had gathered in front of the hotel to help us unpack and carry us and our luggage into the lobby.

We went to Venice, Florence, Rome. In Rome, Douglas engaged a learned professor of archaeology who not only knew his subject but a little English in the bargain. One day, in a restaurant, the professor was telling Douglas how every Italian knew and worshiped him. The more he spoke of Douglas and eliminated me from the conversation the more embarrassed Douglas grew. Finally, Douglas stopped him.

"Excuse me, professor," he said, "my wife is equally, if not better known, not only in America, but throughout the world, and that goes for your country too."

Whereupon the professor turned a beaming face on me.

"*Sì, sì*, but of course," he said, "the name of Maria Pinkerton is well known all over Italy."

That was something that Douglas, an incurable tease, never let me live down. For the rest of the trip I remained "Maria Pinkerton."

In Paris, where the French also greeted us with great warmth and enthusiasm, we found ourselves in a suite at the Hôtel Crillon adjoining that of General Pershing.

One afternoon Douglas glanced out the window and quickly turned to me:

"Don't go out on the balcony, Mary! There's a huge crowd in front of the hotel and they're waiting to pay honor to General Pershing."

Later that day Douglas and I had the pleasure of General Pershing's company at tea.

"That was quite a crowd you had this afternoon, you two," he remarked casually.

In a Parisian crowd

"But, General . . . !" Douglas and I spluttered.

"Yes," he went on, "I was smart enough to stay indoors and keep off that balcony. There must have been several thousand people."

Douglas and I looked at one another and burst into astonished laughter. To our bewildered commander in chief we explained that we had done the very same thing.

Our four weeks were now drawing to a close; four weeks in which we had made a trip that should have taken four months. We were so exhausted that we were practically carried on the boat. There we had our first real rest.

220

All through the trip, on the train, in New York, during the crossing to England, on the automobile trip through the Continent, I had been begging Douglas to read a magazine story that had been submitted for his approval. I had read it on the voyage over and was most enthusiastic.

"If you like it that much, Mary," he said, "I'm going to cable them to go right ahead on the script, costumes, and sets."

"No, Douglas, I want you to read it yourself first. I don't relish the responsibility."

Despite my protest he cabled instructions to buy the story, prepare the sets, and make the costumes. But it was not until we were on the train returning to Hollywood that I finally anchored him with the magazine.

"Promise to play two games of hearts with me, Mary, and I'll read it."

"It's a deal. Now . . . not another word till you've finished it."

Douglas read without stopping—right through our dinner hour. The film he made from that story started him on an entirely different trend in picture making. It was *The Mark of Zorro*.

The day-to-day chronicle of our trip through Europe had naturally reached the newspapers at home. Stirring as our reception overseas had been, we found still more heart-warming the welcome given us by the reporters and photographers who were waiting on the dock to meet us. Their friendliness was warm and cheering. If there had been any doubts about our future on the screen, they had been completely dispelled by those four weeks we were away. Most significant of all, to my thinking, had been this: staid Mother England had welcomed the two of us with open arms.

221

Symbolic, too, I believe, was the way in which Owen's mother accepted both the divorce and my remarriage.

Shortly after our return Mrs. Moore paid me a visit at the Pickford-Fairbanks Studio. Without knowing she was there Douglas came into my dressing room. At first he was embarrassed. But Mrs Moore immediately put him at his ease. When I said, "Douglas, I want you to meet Owen's mother," she went up to him, hand outstretched, and said:

"Mr. Fairbanks, I hated you till I realized you were good for my Mary. I only pray that you will live long to protect and care for her. I know you can make her happy."

Douglas thanked her, and I saw tears come to his eyes. Mrs. Moore was right. What Owen had never been to me—companion, helpmeet, teacher, and guide—Douglas now became.

Despite my success I had been a very lonely person. More than anything else I had wanted desperately to be approved of, and that approval Douglas gave me. I had never believed anyone would speak of me and to me as he did. Douglas loved living, and he instilled that into everyone around him. He could never tolerate depressing things, or people. Talk of failure, of sickness, of death was rigorously avoided in his company. Which doesn't mean he was not a loyal friend to people less fortunate than he. To them his loyalty remained unshaken till the day he died. I remember an actor whom Douglas had known well during his years in the theater. This man developed tuberculosis and over a period of twenty-five years Douglas was his sole support. Several times he sent his friend to sanatoriums in Switzerland and other countries. The man was older than Douglas, and, ironically enough, outlived him by several years.

There was one word that always loomed about Douglas in

222

*As a Belgian refugee
in "Through the
Back Door" 1921*

gigantic letters—"Success." Whenever he doodled with pencil
and pad, over a telephone or at a conference table, he would
write those two magic syllables over and over again, in strong
printed letters. When he published his books, they were either
on the theme of "Laugh and Live" or the "Habit of Happiness." So dominant was this creed of success that he drew
successful people to him wherever he went. In fact he almost
seemed to be collecting them.

*I played an Italian lighthouse keeper betrayed
by a German spy in "The Love Light" 1920*

With Charlie and Douglas, 1921

16

One of the most successful people in Douglas' group of early friends was Charlie Chaplin. Charlie was also one of the four original members of United Artists, which included D. W. Griffith, Douglas, and myself. My relation with Charlie over the years has been strange and unpredictable, fluctuating between mutual affection and admiration and intense resentment and hostility. And I want to be very fair in my appraisal of him both as an artist and as a human being. I think that the most moving and human memory I have of Charlie is his grief over Douglas' passing in December 1939. I had called him in Los Angeles from Chicago because of urgent United Artists business, never dreaming that he would come to the phone. I thought I might get the butler and have a message relayed to him. Charlie will rarely if ever answer a telephone, no matter how urgent the call may be. Nor does he ever answer letters. In all the years I have known him I have received just one short note from him.

H

When I made my call, it was ten o'clock in the morning in Chicago, and eight in Los Angeles. To my great surprise Charlie answered the phone himself. I believe he was then working on his picture *The Great Dictator*. We talked for an hour. Charlie reminisced warmly and volubly about the happy days the three of us had spent together. I realized then, perhaps as I had never before, how very deep the friendship of Charlie and Douglas had been.

"I've lost the inspiration and incentive to make pictures, Mary," he said.

"You mustn't say that, Charlie; Douglas would be furious with you."

"You know how much I depended upon his enthusiasm. You remember how I always showed my pictures first to Douglas."

"Yes, Charlie, I can still hear Douglas laughing so heartily he couldn't look at the screen. Remember those coughing fits he'd get at that moment?"

"More than anything else I remember this, Mary: whenever I made a particular scene I would always anticipate the pleasure it would give Douglas."

It all came back to me how Douglas used to treat Charlie like a younger brother, listening patiently and intently, hours on end, to his repetitious stories, which frankly bored me to extinction. Charlie had a way of developing his scenarios by repeating them over and over again to his most intimate friends —testing them privately on people he had faith in. Only then would he put them on film. . . . I heard a catch in Charlie's voice.

"Mary, I couldn't bear to see them put that heavy stone over Douglas."

226

In 1912 I had heard about Charlie Chaplin, but had never seen him, either in person or on the screen. I knew of the furor he had created, but at that time I just thought of him as a pie-throwing comedian. I was at Levy's, one of the two places where we usually dined in Los Angeles, when I saw a dark-eyed figure, with heavy black wavy hair, high starched collar with stock tie, seated alone at a nearby table. My companion leaned toward me.

"Charlie Chaplin," he whispered.

I remember how amazed I was. For one thing, I had expected a much older man. Then, I was totally unprepared for the sensitivity of his face and the smallness of his hands. As I looked in Chaplin's direction a waiter came up behind him and opened a transom, unloosing an avalanche of dust on Charlie's head and into his plate of soup.

Charlie just waved him and the bowl of soup away. There was a touching grace and restraint about his gesture. I would never have recognized the slapstick comedian who looked more like a poet or a violinist.

I didn't meet Charlie until years later. And it wasn't until I married Douglas that the three of us became almost inseparable.

Charlie once engaged a Hawaiian orchestra to come all the way from the other side of Los Angeles to serenade me at Pickfair in the middle of the night. That was one of the weirdest experiences of my life. Charlie was spending the week end with Douglas and me, as was his habit when we had become virtually one family. No invitation was ever needed. He was always welcome to come and play with us, and we were just as happy to have him as he was to be with us. It was a moonlit night, and I was dreaming, dreaming that I was dying to the accompaniment of celestial music. I awakened and couldn't believe my ears. The music seemed to be real. And those four Hawaiian musicians on the lawn below were very real indeed. The next morning as we were talking about it at breakfast, Charlie said:

"You'd never guess, Doug, what was going through my mind while those men were playing."

"Probably a scene from your next picture."

"No, I had a strange vision that Mary was dying. I saw her in bed with the moonlight falling on her face and her long blond hair. . . ."

I gave a shiver.

". . . And I thought what if Mary were really dying and this music was accompanying her exit——"

"Charlie," I said, "you've just made that up. You didn't really imagine it last night!"

"So help me, Mary, it's true!"

"This is the most frightening coincidence! You see, Charlie, I dreamed the very thing you were thinking. I dreamed that I was actually dying."

Whatever the stunt, whatever the prank or practical joke, so long as Charlie was responsible for it, Douglas thought it was great . . . And the two of them would romp all over Pickfair like ten-year-olds. I couldn't count the number of times I stayed behind to entertain one or another of Charlie's wives, while they would go wandering up and down the surrounding hills. Sometimes Charlie's current spouse might not be altogether to my liking, or I to hers; and sometimes there were things I wanted to do around the house—I had such little time away from the studio. But I would dutifully sit with whichever Mrs.

Chaplin it might be and chat amiably till the wanderers strolled in again.

Once they climbed up on the water tower and almost fell in. Douglas, of course, was always climbing, and whoever was with him had to be prepared for some sort of ascent. We were visiting Henry Ford in Pasadena one summer. As it was getting late, I asked the butler if Mr. Fairbanks was ready to go home.

"I don't know, madam," he replied. "They're up there."

I followed the butler's pointing finger and there up on the roof, straddled across the tile and facing each other, were Douglas Fairbanks and Henry Ford. They were engaged in a heated discussion, completely oblivious of where they were. I waited fully an hour before the "boys" clambered down again.

"How in the world did you have the courage to take Mr. Ford up there?" I asked.

"It's all right, Hipper. I rehearsed it three or four times for him and showed him where the handholds were."

What Douglas was on the screen he was in real life. Whatever the danger in any of his films, he never used a double or any precautions. To him that just wasn't cricket. Douglas was always exploring, and playing the prankster.

When the whole motion-picture industry was in the doghouse over some new black sheep, Douglas and Charlie would pick up the telephone and ring up the more pompous and self-righteous movie people and pretend they were newspaper reporters.

"We understand you know a great deal more about this scandal than you've told the police. This story may mean our job; can we quote you to the effect that . . ."

There would be an immediate threat of a lawsuit from the other end of the telephone. Of course I was always listening

With Douglas and Charlie—just clowning

in on an extension. I would get terrified when I heard those indignant tones. I was certain the police would trace the call and the industry would have a fresh scandal on its hands.

Not that Douglas and Charlie were always acting like a couple of kids out of Mark Twain. I saw them once watching Professor Einstein demonstrate his theory of relativity with a knife, a fork, a plate, and the edge of our dining-room table. I can still see the look of complete concentration and befuddlement on their faces.

We were having dinner with Dr. and Mrs. Einstein at Pickfair shortly after they arrived in this country. Professor Einstein's language was then only beginning to take recognizable shape as English, which did not make the theory any clearer. I'm afraid that even if the professor's English had been flawless, we would still have been in the dark, relatively speaking. A brain specialist who was present had at first introduced the subject of thought transference.

"Was is das?" asked Einstein.

"I think and concentrate my thinking on you," explained the brain specialist, "and you catch my thought."

"Nein," said Professor Einstein, "das ist not possible."

"But wasn't your theory just as incredible—and still is to most people?"

Professor Einstein insisted it was really a very simple theory. To prove his point he slapped the edge of the table as the outer rim of space, used the plate as the world or the sun or universe, I can't recall which, and plied away at the fourth dimension with his silverware.

I was too awed to ask questions, so I amused myself by studying the openmouthed attention of Charlie and Douglas.

I have read and heard many harsh things about Charlie, and I've said a few myself. Nor have we ever seen eye to eye politically, but I've always maintained that if people knew something about Charlie's childhood, they would be more tolerant of his singular temperament. When Charlie was only seven years old his mother lost her reason. I'll never forget the time Charlie told me how the children stoned both him and her as he led her by the hand to the hospital. Destitute, their father dead, Charlie and his brother Syd were placed in a workhouse. There they remained for three years. Charlie used to describe the terror he felt when he saw other children being caned.

Charlie had never seen an orange until one bleak, rainy Christmas Day shortly after he was admitted to the workhouse, and oranges were being handed out to the boys. Poor little fellow, he had made a mistake in bed the night before. So when his turn came he reached out for the coveted object, only to be yanked brusquely out of line and told, "You're a nasty little boy, and you don't deserve to have an orange."

"Do you know," Charlie said to me, "I looked at this golden ball of color, so beautiful against the drabness of the uniforms and the gray walls of the workhouse, and I didn't even know an orange was something to eat."

Finally he and his brother ran away, and nearly starved to death on the streets of London. Many a night they spent over the gratings of a bakery, almost driven out of their minds with hunger when they smelled the fresh bread. It was the only warm spot they could find, and they slept with newspapers over them. They managed to earn a few pennies by carving out little toy boats, and, of course, they had to filch their food where they could.

Another singular side of Charlie's temperament, which his childhood explains, was his scornful attitude toward any strong family ties. He knew how much I loved my mother, yet once he said to me, quite seriously:

"That's nothing but spooks, Mary—loving one's family that way."

Yet, however much he might deny the slightest filial attachment, he went to great lengths to bring his stricken mother from

England to California. The few years remaining the poor woman were passed in ease and comfort, but she died never knowing that the world's greatest comedian was her son.

This same sense of loyalty Charlie has shown to innumerable friends, and no one has ever known exactly how many helpless people owe their sole maintenance to him. Many are friends from the lean days whom he has never forsaken. Charlie has been very careful to keep this all to himself.

Wealthy as he is, I believe the specter of poverty still haunts him. I know, too, that for a long time it was a great sorrow to Charlie that he never grew into the tall, romantic type. Douglas and I were in the living room of Pickfair one day. Charlie was studying himself in the glass, and we both heard him say, more to himself than to us:

"My head is too big for my body; my arms are too short for my body; and my hands are too small for my arms."

"What about me?" I said, showing him my reflection beside his. "My head is too big for my body and my arms are too long for it. And I'm a woman, Charlie."

On another occasion Charlie drew a tattered newspaper article out of his pocket and handed it to us.

"I want you both to read this," he said.

Douglas and I expected at the very least to find some kind words about Charlie's gift for pantomime. Imagine our astonishment when we read the most scathing denunciation of Charlie Chaplin we had ever seen in print. Among other things it said that Charlie was the result of "generations of underfed guttersnipes." The rest was in that redolent vein.

"You see," he said as we read the clipping in dismay, "not everyone thinks *as well* of me as you do."

Douglas let him have it.

"Charlie," he said, "you've got to throw that disgusting tripe away! Of all the wonderful things people have written about you, why should you treasure that rot?"

And I added, "Only some mean person suffering from envy and resentment could have written that, Charlie. Why must you hug a viper to your heart? If you must carry a clipping in your pocket, select one that can inspire you."

Charlie was unshakable. Evidently he found some twisted satisfaction in this vicious attack on everything he stood for in the pantomimic art of the screen.

"No," he said, "I'm holding on to that article, because it tells the truth, not the whole truth, I admit. That man, unfair as he is, says many things about me that are correct, and I must never forget them."

With that he put the clipping in his pocket, and Douglas and I knew it was useless to go on arguing with him. Real humility, however, is not part of Charlie's make-up, certainly not as regards his art. I believe he knows he is the world's greatest comedian. I, of course, agree with him.

Profoundly as I respect Charlie Chaplin's talents and much as I valued his early friendship, nothing in the world would induce me to live over the agonizing years I experienced with Charlie as a business partner. As a co-owner of United Artists, I was convinced we could survive only by continually modernizing our setup. This Charlie would not permit.

"Charlie," I would say, "we ought to streamline the company and keep with the general trend of the times."

But there was no moving him. I don't think Charlie knew himself what he wanted. I finally became convinced he just didn't want what I wanted, that, somehow, particularly after Douglas' death, I rubbed him the wrong way. It finally came to this: no matter what I proposed, or how I proposed it, Charlie would automatically, without giving the matter any consideration, flatly turn it down. As we were 50-50 partners I was completely stymied. The inevitable, of course, happened. United Artists faced bankruptcy. I gave my power of attorney to Joseph Schenck, whom I trusted implicitly as a friend and businessman. I shall never forget the day I went to Charlie's home to urge him to do the same. I thought I had seen Charlie in a tantrum, but this beat everything. *

"I wouldn't give my power of attorney to my own brother," he shouted. "I'm perfectly capable of voting my own stock."

"But, Charlie, you know Schenck is a good businessman."

"I'm as good a businessman as anybody else!"

Of course poor Charlie was no businessman at all. I appealed to his sense of fair play and sportsmanship.

"Charlie," I said, "I'm not here as your partner today. I'm not even here as someone that's been your friend for so many years. I'm here as the voice of our thousands of employees the world over, of the producers and bankers——"

At that word he cut me short.

"If you're here as the voice of the bankers the interview is terminated."

"Very well, Charlie," I said, and without another word from either of us I started for the door.

I saw that he had no intention of opening it for me, and I prayed not to lose my temper. Of course, as luck would have it, something was wrong with the lock, for the door wouldn't give. So Charlie had to let me out after all.

United Artists meeting, 1936. Douglas Fairbanks, Jr.,
Charlie Chaplin, Sam Goldwyn, Jock Whitney,
David O. Selznick, Walter Wanger, Jesse L. Lasky,
and Douglas Fairbanks, Sr.

At length, after years of continual wrangling, in February 1951 we finally sat down in a conference room one day and signed over the company to six young men who then had the power to put United Artists back on its feet. And that was the last time I saw that obstinate, suspicious, egocentric, maddening, and lovable genius of a problem child, Charlie Chaplin.

236

17

In some ways Charlie Chaplin's early life reminded me of my own. I, too, had experienced extreme poverty. And, like Charlie, I'd never really known what it meant to be a child. I sometimes feel that my only real childhood was lived through the many children's roles I played, even into adulthood.

There was Rebecca. . . .

I was twenty-two years old when I played that unforgettable little eleven-year-old from Sunnybrook Farm. But I enjoyed the part as if I were still a child myself.

"Rebecca," said her mother, "you have a hole in the back of your stocking."

And Rebecca did what I had once done myself before leaving for Sunday school. She dashed back into the house and put shoe polish over the hole in her black stocking.

And there was the pie-eating episode in which she said to her aunt:

"Is that great big piece of pie for Aunt Miranda?"

"No, Rebecca, it's for you."

"Golly me, what a little bit!"

So she wasn't allowed to eat any pie at all, but told to clear the table and return to the pantry with the luscious blackberry pie. And she reached for the piece that was meant for her, but as it got close to her mouth her eyes wandered to the wall, and there staring her in the face, and framed in large accusing letters, was the sampler with the commandment "Thou Shalt Not Steal." Rebecca dropped the piece of pie like a hot coal and was wiping her hands on her apron, when she saw, on the opposite wall, a second homemade motto, and this one read, "God Helps Those Who Help Themselves." That was a philosophy she agreed with wholeheartedly. She retrieved the large slice of pie and with an easy conscience proceeded to consume it.

I shall always remember the role of Rebecca for another reason. It was while I was making this film that we entered World War I. Like many actors at that time, Douglas and Charlie Chaplin and I made a great many speeches for the Liberty Loan Drive.

In Washington, D.C., I remember, the three of us and that beloved comedienne, Marie Dressler, were invited to the White House. Those who recall the austere Mr. Woodrow Wilson will understand my chagrin, not to mention Charlie's and Douglas', when Marie told him a story that was not exactly risqué, but definitely off color. As she moved to the denouement, I kept wishing the parquet floor of the Blue Room would open up and swallow me. I could feel myself blushing all over. The President neither smiled nor made a comment. We were all overawed by our first visit to the White House, all but Marie,

At left, Franklin Delano Roosevelt; kneeling, Marie Dressler and Charlie Chaplin; behind them, Douglas and I; at right, Mother. Washington, 1918

the darling. She remained sublimely unconscious of her *faux pas.* Mr. Tumulty, the President's secretary, introduced us to the then Assistant Secretary of the Navy, a tall, slender, and bespectacled young man by the name of Franklin Delano Roosevelt. Later that day we all met in front of the Treasury for the official opening of the drive. The streets were thick with people watching the colorful parade, which came to a halt on the steps of the Treasury, where we made more speeches to open the nationwide campaign.

It was then that Marie Dressler had another undignified encounter with a president, this time a president-to-be. During the ceremonies on the Treasury steps Mr. Roosevelt tripped and fell through the railing on the stand. The buxom Marie proceeded to fall right on top of him. At the White House in 1933 President Roosevelt asked me if I remembered the episode. I told him I most certainly did.

"I've a photograph of all of us together that day," he said. "Would you like a copy?"

Naturally I did, and I am happy at the chance now to reproduce it.

I raised $5,000,000 in one afternoon and evening in Pittsburgh during the Liberty Bond Drive. The most arduous if not the most productive day of all was in Baltimore. I sold only $450,000 in bonds, but they were almost entirely in small denominations of fifty and one hundred dollars. That little marathon took from nine in the morning till twelve midnight. Mother phrased it quite aptly when she remarked at the end of the tour that "we lived on coffee and handshakes."

Another child's role that I played when I was an adult was Sara Crewe of *The Little Princess*.

I was supposed to look like a girl of eight or ten. In order to create the illusion of a small child everything I touched had to be a third bigger than life. That was the first time artificial proportion was used on the screen. If I touched a glass it would be a third larger than any actual glass. Knobs of doors were both larger and higher, and of course the people I worked with were selected for their abnormal height. I believe the men averaged six feet three or four. Of course there was the initial advantage of my being rather small myself.

It was in *The Little Princess* that my director Marshall (Mickey) Neilan began using off-stage tricks to get me into the right humor for a scene. Zasu Pitts was playing a scullery maid in that film, her first important assignment on the screen. There was one scene where it was important to catch the slow spread of laughter on my face as I turned suddenly and caught Zasu going through a comical routine of being a grand lady. Mickey wanted to photograph the laughter being born in my eyes, from the first blank surprise to the final hilarious outburst.

In the midst of that crescendo of mirth out pranced Charlie Chaplin and my brother Jack, draped in mounts of artificial flowers and pieces of old lace and ribbon; Jack with a hideous hemp wig which he had on backwards. Safe from the eye of the camera, but within the range of my own, they proceeded to do a spring dance—cavorting about with trouser legs rolled up, while Mickey whistled Mendelssohn's "Spring Song"!

I think Mickey was satisfied with the results.

In the film *Stella Maris* I played *two* young girls.

I was the crippled rich girl Stella, who knew nothing of death, poverty, sickness, or war, nothing of man's inhumanity to man; who lived in a tower overlooking the sea and whose only friends were the sea gulls. And Unity Blake, who knew

241

all the black things that were kept from Stella, yet could still laugh.

I figured that Unity Blake would probably have one shoulder dropped and one hip high from having carried younger children on the other hip in her formative years. That was the way I walked as Unity. When another company later made *Stella Maris*, they gave the actress a lumpy rubber suit to wear. That was grotesque, because actually Unity was not deformed. As Unity, I also plastered my hair with Vaseline to take out the curls and make it look dark and scraggly in contrast to Stella's curls. I can never forget the moment when Unity, in love with the same man as Stella, stares at herself forlornly in the mirror.

"Well, I've got pretty hair too," she says.

And staring back at her, in mocking rebuttal, is a mop of ugly hair, and under it a plain and unattractive face. Slowly the tears stream down that homely little face, and Unity buries her head in her hands. I could cry now when I think of that girl. Mother came into my bedroom one morning before I left for the studio, and looked at me gravely.

"Mary," she said, "you've actually grown to look like Unity."

And I had. Adolph Zukor, who was in Hollywood at the time, came in to see me one day when I was dressed as Unity. The look of dismay on the poor man's face was something to see. I had to pacify him by assuring him that I died very early in the picture.

"The sooner the better!" said Mr. Zukor.

I also played an ugly little girl in *Suds*—a film I remember best for its other leading character—a dejected, downtrodden, world-weary horse named Lavender. For weeks the studio

242

As Unity Blake in "Stella Maris" 1918

"Suds"
1920

hunted for a suitably dejected horse for the part. When they found him, he was working on a sand pile near Los Angeles more dead than alive. For his role in *Suds,* Lavender was promoted from a sand pile to pulling a laundry wagon.

In a memorable sequence Lavender, trudging heavily uphill, is suddenly dragged back by the load, smashes the wagon, spilling the clean laundry all over a muddy street. His owner, an irate laundress, sells him to a glue factory. As Lavender's closest friend, I fly to the rescue, arriving in the nick of time with the reprieve. I take Lavender to my boardinghouse and tie him to a lamppost outside. It begins to pour; I sneak him upstairs to my bedroom on an outside staircase. Lavender starts to caper around; the ceiling of the apartment below falls on the gathered heads of the landlord's family. Lavender and I are thrown out into the street, where a policeman arrests me. A rich lady comes in a Rolls-Royce, pays my fine, and offers to take Lavender to her country estate. I agree. She invites me for the week end and I have my last meeting with Lavender. Assuming that my old friend will remember me, I leap on his back. But Lavender is so full of the joy of life that he bucks me off in the middle of a stream. As a hurt expression comes over my face, the last title of the picture reads:

"That's gratitude for you."

Since Lavender wasn't needed during the first two weeks of the picture, we put him in Douglas' stables across the street from our studio. There some cowboys promised to take good care of him, along with our Western ponies. Two weeks later, on the morning of Lavender's debut before the camera, the property boy dashed into the studio pale as death.

"I have terrible news for you, Miss Pickford!"

245

"You don't have to tell me," I cried. "Lavender is dead!"

"Worse!" said the property boy. "Come here and look!"

Outside in the sunlight was Lavender—a heavier and healthier Lavender by sixty pounds, cantering along like a two-year-old.

"What am I going to do?" whispered the property boy, certain he would lose his job for failing to tell the cowboys that they should not feed Lavender too many oats.

I told the property boy not to worry, but to give me a hand at disguising Lavender's new-found health. In those days, aging actors with a generous allotment of chin would often deftly apply rouge to conceal the offending surplus. I thought to myself, "If that applies to actors' chins, why can't I do it to Lavender's stomach?"

With the help of our frightened property boy I painted Lavender's stomach and lined his sides with gray streaks to make it appear that his ribs were standing out. Then I proceeded to paint shadows under his eyes, and, to make him look more lugubrious, we ruffled up his tail. Thus made up, Lavender made a brilliant debut on the screen as the underfed and bedraggled horse he was supposed to be in the first place.

I was twenty-seven years old when I played one of my most successful children—Little Lord Fauntleroy. In this film I also portrayed little Lord Fauntleroy's mother. Nowadays trick photography, trick sets, and parallel takes are a commonplace, but in those days every new device was an adventure, every new camera angle a discovery.

People were baffled that I looked nine inches taller as the mother than I did as the boy.

"Little Lord Fauntleroy" 1921

Three of those inches came from an elevated ramp on which I walked whenever Little Lord Fauntleroy was beside me. I got my idea for the remaining six inches from a practice adopted centuries ago by some enterprising young ladies of Venice. I had read that they used to wear shoes that gave them a height they thought more appropriate to their rank. So I had a pair of these "platforms" made. I remember with what anxiety I descended a staircase. We took one scene over several times, because three or four times my footing gave way, and once I fell nearly the whole length of the stairs. The scene in which "Dearest" kisses her son took us fifteen hours to accomplish. It lasted exactly three seconds on the screen!

When I look back over the children's roles I have played, there is one I always remember with a slight shudder. That is "M'liss." . . .

As the fearless, trusted friend of forest creatures, I had to play two scenes in this film that demanded some of the realest acting of my career. One was a scene in which M'liss was supposed to give three chocolate caramels to a monstrous bear. It was a very hot day, I remember. And when little M'liss offered the bear the first chocolate caramel something went wrong. The camera buckled. As the men started to reload the film magazines, I stood by, quiet and nervous, my hand closed around the chocolates. In the meantime the bear was on a leash held by his trainer. Finally the camera began grinding again, and the bear came toward me. I opened my hand, expecting him to pick up the caramels daintily, one by one. To my dismay they were one large syrupy smear, running through my fingers and around to the back of my hand. There was nothing I could do, for the bear was already licking my palm. Next, he turned my hand

248

With Thomas Mieghan in "M'liss" 1918

over with his long claws and licked the back of it. Finally he was licking between my fingers.

Nor was this bear episode all they cooked up for M'liss. "I've got a surprise for you today, Tad," the director, Mickey Neilan, using a nickname for me, said. On the floor of the set was a huge wooden box that I hadn't seen there the day before. Knowing what a prankster he was, I watched suspiciously as he lifted the lid of the box. To my horror a five-foot snake raised its head and looked me straight in the eye.

"Mickey, you're mad!" I cried, backing away.

"Easy, easy, Tad," he said, "it's not poisonous. I want you to pick it up."

This was one time I was not going to obey orders. I was opening my mouth in indignant protest when I saw a smirk on the face of a studio carpenter, as much as to say, "Just as I thought —a scared cat. So, without a whimper, I allowed Mickey to put my index finger on the snake, and gradually I had all five fingers around its body. I remember how surprised I was that it didn't feel slimy. It was just cold in a smooth, uniform way, and I was amazed at the muscular reaction of the body.

In the actual filming the snake wound itself around my arm and coyly tucked its tail up under my tattered sleeve! That scene, I learned later, was put in the picture on a wager. It was not in the script. Mickey Neilan had had an overnight inspiration. When he confided the plan to the staff the following morning, they ridiculed him, saying he could never persuade me to do it. He bet—and won.

Every now and then, as the years went by and I continued to play children's roles, it would worry me that I was becom-

ing a personality instead of an actress. I would suddenly resent the fact that I had allowed myself to be hypnotized by the public into remaining a little girl. A wild impulse would seize me to reach for the nearest shears and remove that blond chain around my neck. It was sometime in 1922 that rebellion led me to a somewhat disastrous action. I read *Dorothy Vernon of Haddon Hall* and decided this would not only be my next part but my farewell to childhood on the screen. I could think of no more fitting role for promotion to young womanhood.

My first taste of ill-luck came when I brought Ernst Lubitsch from Germany to direct me. The power and originality of his work had already spread far and wide. But for many at that time he was still the "Hun," and I soon found myself being denounced almost as a traitor for ignoring our own directors in favor of the erstwhile enemy.

But that was nothing compared to what followed. Mr. Lubitsch had read the script in German and consented to direct the picture. For some unknown reason, upon his arrival in Hollywood, he changed his mind. Mr. Lubitsch spoke very broken English at the time, but his meaning was far from broken, because it was the blunt and inescapable truth.

"Der iss too many qveens and not enough qveens!"

What he meant, and he was absolutely right, was that the story of Queen Elizabeth and Mary, Queen of Scots, was so much bigger than Dorothy Vernon's; that it would have been better to drop Dorothy entirely, the only other alternative being to eliminate the queens. Mr. Lubitsch was most apologetic, but nothing could persuade him to direct the picture. So we had to shelve *Dorothy Vernon* for the time being. And here was Ernst Lubitsch, an idle genius in Hollywood. We put our heads together and the result was *Rosita*—the worst picture, bar none, that I ever made. In Europe, Lubitsch's reputation had been built on sophisticated comedies, more than slightly on the risqué side. In line with this I tried to make Rosita very correct but a little naughty too, and the result was disastrous.

Almost the only compensation I derived from Rosita was a small amount of comedy relief I enjoyed at Mr. Lubitsch's expense while we were making the picture.

"Rosita" 1922

With Charlie and Douglas in 1922.
The set of "Rosita" is in the background.

There was a particularly embarrassing moment in the big cathedral scene, where, by arrangement of the king I marched to the altar to be married to a great don. About two hundred extras and one hundred technicians were on the set while I waited, seated in my portable dressing room for my cue. Mr. Lubitsch clapped for silence, and in the awesome interior of the great cathedral set I suddenly heard him say in a loud and commanding voice:

"Qviet, please! This is the scenes vehr Miss Pickford goes mit the beckside to ze altar."

There was a moment of agonized silence; then a half-stifled

254

giggle, and finally a volley of laughter boomed through the cathedral. I told my maid to explain to Mr. Lubitsch that that was not the most reverent way of describing my approach to the altar. Poor, dear Ernst—I never saw a man so covered with confusion as when my Alsatian maid, with motions and what not, conveyed my message to him. He came over hurriedly and begged my pardon.

"Is it correct English to say," he asked. " 'This is the scenes vehr Miss Pickford goes mit the beck to ze altar?' "

"Perfectly correct English," I assured him.

And, with a very worried look, he said, "Not unpolite?"

"Not unpolite."

With that Mr. Lubitsch gave the amended instructions, in a less commanding voice this time, and I sallied forth from my dressing room to proceed down the cathedral aisle "mit the beck to ze altar."

So much for *Rosita*—my first punishment for wanting to grow up on the screen. But I still wasn't convinced. Lubitsch or no Lubitsch, I now decided to do *Dorothy Vernon of Haddon Hall*. I discussed it with my old friend and director, Mickey Neilan, who didn't mind the "too many qveens and not enough qveens," and he it was who finally directed the film. That picture cost me $1,000,000 to make. It wasn't too badly received by the press. Many people even professed to love it. But I knew something for certain now: the public just refused to accept me in any role older than the gawky, fighting age of adolescent girlhood. *Dorothy Vernon* was infinitely better than *Rosita*—almost any film could have been—but not in the same class, either in merit or box-office success, with *Rebecca* or *Little Lord Faunt-*

As "Dorothy Vernon of Haddon Hall"

leroy. On top of all that I suffered almost the greatest fright of my life while making this picture.

The whole episode began rather embarrassingly in Golden Gate Park, San Francisco, where about ten thousand spectators had gathered to watch us take a scene of me riding a beautiful white horse named Pearl. To the great amusement of the crowd I was unable to lift myself into the stirrup because of a very elegant brocaded velvet costume which weighed over thirty-five pounds. The crowd volunteered various ways of helping me out of my predicament.

"How about a stepladder! Let's give you a boost, Mary!"

In the end the upholstery had to go, and I was obliged to put on a dress of lighter weight, the next problem was that the horse might slip on the asphalt road we had selected for the scene. To prevent this, we put four rubber shoes on Pearl.

I was riding along at increasing speed, side by side with a car containing the cameraman and his assistant, director Neilan and his assistant, and a technician, when I suddenly heard them shrieking at me in one voice.

Pearl, it seems, had cast off one of the rubber shoes from a hind hoof. Panic-stricken, she began to race like mad trying to outdistance the car. To add to her panic, I was, of course, riding sidesaddle, to which I was totally unaccustomed, and twenty-odd pounds of multiple skirt were flapping wildly in the wind over her flank.

The risk of a sudden fall was very great indeed, and I could understand the wild shouting and gesticulating of the men in the car. I tried to remain calm, because I knew better than they did what would happen if I lost my head. I shouted back to them to reduce their speed gradually.

With Anders Randolph in
"Dorothy Vernon of Haddon Hall"

Directly ahead of me was an intersecting highway, with automobiles racing in both directions. Pearl was throwing out her
front feet, head low, blindly plunging toward that highway. I
got way up in the saddle, right over her ears, and started talking
to her. She and I were alone now.

"That's all right, Pearl," I said.

She had belonged to two other women before, so she was at
least accustomed to a female voice. I went on talking into her
ear; patting and smoothing her neck, calming her as best I

258

could; while ever so gently I pulled in the reins. I knew that if I reined her in too quickly, she would rear in the air and throw the two of us. Between patting and stroking and assuring Pearl that she was a good girl I managed to mumble to myself, "Please, God, help us!"

Just as we reached the intersection, I gave the reins a quick jerk with both my hands, and Pearl reared, half stumbled, and landed in a culvert on all fours. I am proud to say I did not lose my seat.

Automobiles had started putting on brakes, and you can imagine the amazement of those men and women as Dorothy Vernon of Haddon Hall came tearing out of nowhere on a white horse, blond curls flying in the wind, garbed in an elaborate Elizabethan robe. Poor Pearl was drenched in perspiration, and so terrified that the veins and muscles were standing out like whipcords all over her body. I've never seen five more frightened human beings than the men in that camera car.

You would suppose that that was excitement enough for one picture. Another little picnic awaited me a few scenes later, when it was necessary to negotiate a leap on horseback up a narrow stone stairway and along a three-foot-wide, ten-foot-high wall. Even Mickey Neilan thought that stunt too hazardous for an amateur like me. So he very thoughtfully engaged an expert horsewoman to undertake it as my double. The inevitable happened. At the last moment my double's horse sprained its ankle. I offered her the use of Pearl, but she refused.

"This is a strange horse," she said, "I can't take a chance."

"Will you do it, Mary?" Mickey Neilan asked me.

259

In those days none of us ever thought of protesting over a matter of life and limb. The director's word was law.

While we shot that scene, I was for some reason abnormally calm. Pearl must have sensed the calm, because, all the way up those stone steps and over that narrow wall, with the cameras going, she wasn't the slightest bit nervous. I came off unscathed; indeed the only hurt I suffered was when I learned, from an article in one of the movie magazines, that it was my double, and not I, who rode the horse in that scene!

It was during the filming of *Dorothy Vernon* that I discovered I could relax, in the midst of the greatest commotion, by going to sleep in any costume and in almost any position. A cameraman said to me one day, "Miss Pickford, you have three minutes before you're needed on the stage." I made up my mind to use those three minutes to best advantage. I was caparisoned in one of the weightiest attires that was ever loaded upon this puny frame of mine. There was a liquid powder on my hands. Every hair on my head was meticulously in place. All this had to be perfect the moment the director's voice boomed out and cameras began to grind. I signaled the wardrobe woman, who put a Japanese pillow under my head (the Japanese use a small block of wood) and a folded towel on my chest to prevent the powder from spotting my gown. Then she pulled my skirts straight under me in order not to wrinkle them, and in all that noise and hammering, with cameramen and carpenters yelling to one another, I lay perfectly flat and slept.

When I awoke from that brief but profound snooze, and went on stage, the cameraman studied my face.

In 1926 Douglas was producing
"The Black Pirate," and I "Sparrows"

"What did you put in your eyes, Miss Pickford?" he said.
"Why do you ask?"
"They're so bright!"
"Oh, I just slept."

After *Rosita* and *Dorothy Vernon*, I was quite ready to surrender to public demand and become a child again. My two adventures in adulthood had been costly and embarrassing, but instructive, too. Reacting perhaps against the romantic pretensions of these films, I had a longing to play something human and warm and amusing—something also a little tragic. My choice was *Little Annie Roonie*.

For all the tomboy fun and deviltry and satisfaction of again being among children *Little Annie Roonie* had its tragic side for both me and Annie. I thought it just a little excessive of the director this time to shout out at the blackest moment in little Annie's life:

"All right, boys, get out the rubber boots, Mary has got to cry!"

And how I cried! I was that motherless girl receiving the news that her policeman father had been killed in a gun battle with thugs. I imagined what life would be like without him. . . . This was supposed to be his birthday. I had knitted him a tie with the stripes going in all directions, and he would never wear it now; I had fussed so tenderly over the birthday cake with all the different-size candles sticking up out of it, some long, some short, some skinny, some fat, my idea of a perfect birthday cake, and he would never see it or eat it.

As Mama Molly in "Sparrows" 1926

In "Little Annie Roonie"
1925

Douglas visits my set
during shooting of
"Little Annie Roonie"

While we were taking that scene Rudolph Valentino unexpectedly walked in on the set one day with a friend from Europe.
At any other time his presence would have been thrilling and
welcome; but that afternoon it threw me emotionally off balance. It took me hours to get back into the mood of the tragedy
of that little girl of twelve. Had it been make-believe and nothing more, I could have turned it on and off at will. But I really
was that bereaved little orphan.

264

My brother Jack, Marie Duchess de Gramont,
myself, and Douglas at our studio in 1923

18

I was home at Pickfair, enjoying a day off from *Little Annie Roonie* when Douglas telephoned.

"Where are you?" he asked solemnly.

"I'm rowing down Hollywood Boulevard in a golden gondola."

"This is serious, Mary," he said impatiently. "What part of the house are you in?"

I said, "The upper hall."

"All right. Now listen carefully! Call the butler and the gardener and tell them not to leave the house. Go immediately to your own room and lock the door. Do you hear?"

"Yes, Douglas, but what's it all about . . . ?" I asked, more puzzled than frightened.

"I can't explain now. I'm leaving the studio and coming right out. Please do as I say!"

From the tone of Douglas' voice I knew now it was no light matter. Still it was curiosity rather than fear that was uppermost in my mind when, twelve to fifteen minutes later, Douglas arrived. With him was the Chief of Police. Then I was scared.

"Mary," said Douglas, "the police have just got wind of a plot to kidnap you and hold you for ransom."

It sounded unreal, like something out of a third-rate Hollywood script. The Chief of Police then explained that I was to be the first of five victims. Next in line were Jackie Coogan, the grandson of a prominent Los Angeles banker, a grandson of an oil tycoon, and finally Pola Negri.

"But how do you know this?" I asked. "And why haven't the men been arrested?"

The Chief replied that he had befriended one of the four men who had turned stool pigeon. There being no concrete evidence against the conspirators, the police now waited for an overt act. The men were plotting in a hotel room in the slum area of Los Angeles. An adjoining room had been rented by the police to keep them under observation.

"We can't close in on them till they make a move, Miss Pickford," said the Chief of Police. "Your job will be to act as if nothing is going on. Stick to your usual schedule. Go and come from the studio at the same hours. Do everything to throw off suspicion that they are being watched. The moment they strike we'll be there to nab them."

I began telling the Chief I was prepared to co-operate to the fullest extent, when Douglas broke in excitedly:

"Chief, I've got to insist on one thing, a bodyguard for Mary!"

"But that would give the game away . . . having him ride around with her."

"Suppose we use him only on the set—and not tell anyone but the head property man. . . ." I suggested.

That was agreed to. A big, jovial, heavy-set detective was introduced by me at the studio the following day as "Mr. Jones." Everybody was puzzled, since we were one close family, working together ten to twelve hours a day, with no secrets kept from one another. And now, out of nowhere, came this mysterious stranger who proceeded to make the studio his home. There was tremendous curiosity, but I gave only discreet, noncommittal replies to their questions. One day "Mr. Jones" carelessly mounted a high stool, and as his coat parted, there was a .38 revolver in full view of everyone on the set. There were no further inquiries as to "Mr. Jones's" identity.

Now began a period of nerve-wracking tension, waiting for those men to act and wondering what form it would take. During this whole period I was never alone for a second. Every day for two weeks the kidnapers came in their car and parked a few blocks from the studio. I generally drove to the studio in a small, glass-enclosed 1924 Rolls-Royce roadster. It was a miniature car, the last word in daintiness, with room for just two people. Only two others like it were ever made: one for the then Prince of Wales, the second for Lady Mountbatten. Douglas had to get permission from both other owners to have a third built for me.

I should like to pay tribute here to my heroic young stand-in, Crete Sykle, who, I found out later, was used as a decoy during those two tense weeks. While I was on the set, Crete, dressed in my hat and coat drove around in the little Rolls-Royce. She was fully aware of the danger, having been told that the police and the kidnapers might start shooting at each other. For some reason the kidnapers never followed her. The police went on keeping tabs on the plotters.

On leaving the studio at night my job was to watch for the police. Douglas and I would drive a couple of blocks in the Rolls-Royce, and the police, using a different car each time, would fall in behind us and follow us to Pickfair. During those anxious two weeks the Shriners held their annual convention in Los Angeles. That gave the kidnapers a brilliant idea. They now began to wear Shriners' hats and put Shriners' banners on their car. If they grabbed me and I screamed for help, people would think it was just a group of Shriners who had been celebrating a little too freely. Finally the kidnapers were observed purchasing a gun; then they rented a house in the Mexican quarters, where they planned to hold all five victims. The police now had all the evidence they needed, but they still wanted an open attempt to move in for the kill. . . .

The brain of the conspiracy was an automobile salesman, an ex-lieutenant of World War I. It was the demonstrating car he used in his work that was parked a few blocks away from our studio during those two weeks. One of his accomplices was a young man who had worked for Wells, Fargo. Another was an ex-butcher who had boasted earlier that he was never late on a job. When asked what he would have done if I had pulled a gun on him, he said he would have "dropped" me without a moment's hesitation.

The climax came unexpectedly one night. Douglas and I had slipped into our automobile and, as usual, looked around for the police car. Suddenly I noticed a convertible some distance down the street. The storm curtains were up, and the men in the car kept peeking from the back. I called Douglas' attention to this as we began moving west on Sunset Boulevard.

270

"I'll keep my eye on it, Mary," he said. "Hów about the police car? Do you see it anywhere?"

After looking all around I reported there was no sign of it. Sunset Boulevard in Beverly Hills is a wide highway, divided in the middle by stretches of lawn. In order to keep the convertible in view Douglas pulled to the left, and we were both soon racing along the boulevard at high speed. Since our Rolls-Royce was of English make, the wheel was on the right-hand side, bringing Douglas that much closer than me to the mysterious convertible. Between us on the seat lay a sawed-off double-barrel shotgun, which I'm told has the kick of a mule. Near it was a .45 Colt. Douglas now began talking to me in feverish tones.

"If the shooting starts, Mary, drop to the floor of the car!"

Several times in my life, in situations of acute stress, I have known a great calm of cold logic and calculation. This was such a moment. It suddenly struck me that Douglas' thinking was not sound. If he were shot going at that speed, I reasoned, the car would crash like a cannon ball and there wouldn't be much left of me, whether I was on the floor or sitting bolt upright. Moreover I wanted to take my chances with him. So while I assured him I would obey, I had already formed a plan of my own. When and if the firing started I would kneel down, place the .45 Colt on the wheel, and get a bead on the driver of the convertible racing to the right of us.

Douglas had taught me to handle a gun, and if I say it with pardonable pride, I'm at least an average shot. This was proved one Fourth of July, when our day watchman failed to hit a target at 150 yards, whereas I got two bull's-eyes, and the remaining shots within two or three of the center circles of the target.

. . . The watchman, I might add, was removed to the studio, where he proved far more useful in the property department. . . .

We were now doing all of eighty miles an hour. I kept telling Douglas not to get ahead of the other car, but he was frightfully excited, and evidently didn't hear me. Douglas swerved sharply to the other side of Sunset Boulevard ahead of the convertible, and in so doing cut directly into the path of a shining brand-new Ford, set, like all other Fords of that period, high from the road. I saw it rock perilously from side to side, and for a moment I was sure it would capsize.

Finally we drove into the Beverly Hills Hotel, followed by the convertible. Frantically Douglas jammed the brakes, jumped out, as the car was still rolling, and, with the sawed-off shotgun cocked, planted himself in the path of our pursuers and shouted:

"Throw up your hands!"

A terrified cry came from the mysterious convertible:

"Stop, Douglas, we're the police! The kidnapers were in the Ford you almost turned over."

Douglas was bathed in cold perspiration and as white as death.

"I will not subject my wife to any more of this danger," he said to the police. "I insist that you arrest those men immediately. I also insist that my wife not be there when you do it."

When the men appeared at the studio the following day a small, slightly built detective named Raymond was there waiting for them. One of the men was in the car and two others were standing near it. The fourth, the stool pigeon, wasn't with them that day. Raymond said to Douglas:

"Watch me slug them."

And without further ado he marched up to the man in the car and knocked him unconscious with the butt of his gun. Then, with the gun pointed, he walked over to the other two and said:

"Will you take it the hard way or will you come quietly?"

Raymond handcuffed both of them, walked back to the car with them, handcuffed the unconscious man, and drove to the studio gates, where Douglas, his brother, his manager, my manager, and several other members of our joint staffs were waiting. Raymond, in cowboy fashion, took out a paper and tobacco and rolled a cigarette with one hand, and Douglas was surprised to see that it wasn't shaking at all. On Douglas' orders I had missed the final act of the drama. When Douglas came to tell me that I was free again to come and go to the studio as I saw fit, I amazed myself and him by breaking down completely. I suppose the tension finally snapped. I suddenly trembled all over and had myself a good hard feminine cry.

When I faced my would-be abductors in court, I was curious to know what their reactions would be upon seeing me for the first time off the screen. The ex-butcher sat opposite the door through which I entered. In his middle thirties, blue-eyed, and ruddy of complexion, he was the last person anyone would cast in such a vicious role. I remember he leaned forward and looked at me with the most friendly expression. The second man was as white as his collar and his eyes were staring-mad. The automobile salesman was only a little less nervous, though he looked me steadily in the eye.

Their attorney, an insignificant pipsqueak of a man, tried to win the jury's sympathy by comparing my Rolls-Royce with the humble vehicle in which his clients were driving. To the annoyance of the judge I proceeded to give him a good tongue-lashing, stating that my husband had bought the Rolls-Royce with hard-earned money, while they had stolen their "humble vehicle."

The judge rapped me to silence, and I glared at the attorney and the three felons whom he was defending with heartbreaking eloquence. I think in sentencing them the law was lenient in the extreme.

The experience left me more cautious than it found me. We now have watchmen day and night, together with every possible police protection—and, I might add, a squad of well-trained watchdogs at Pickfair.

With Douglas and Maurice Chevalier in Paris, 1924

19

After our hectic and exhausting honeymoon traveling with Douglas became an annually observed
ritual. Every spring, summer, or the moment, in fact, a new
film was finished, the trunks were packed and off we went on
another world tour. Europe, Africa, Japan, China, anywhere
there were still faces and places Douglas had not seen.

I shall never forget our visit to Russia in 1926; the under-
cover warnings we received against going; the precautions urged
upon us as we moved into the terra incognita of the revolution;
the secret provisions made to escape by plane if things got hot;
the comic-opera alarms of Douglas—and here as everywhere
else the touching and overwhelming affection of the people.

Invited by Sovkino, which represented the Russian film industry, we arrived in Warsaw five days after a bloody uprising
in which hundreds of people had been slain. The Polish capital
was in deep mourning, the streets empty except for the dismal
funeral carriage that rumbled past our hotel. In our party, be-

sides myself, were Douglas, his brother Robert, his brother's wife Lo Rie, our European representative, and Douglas' personal secretary. We weren't in Warsaw more than an hour when two well-dressed men bearing letters of introduction to Douglas, called upon us. They walked from one room to the next, carefully sniffed into every corner, closed each door behind them as they went through, reopened the hall door and peered out, and then solemnly regarded the two of us.

"Do you really intend to take Madame Mary Pickford into Russia?" one of them asked Douglas.

Douglas said, "Yes."

"You are not afraid?"

"No. Should I be?"

"We have come for the special purpose of warning you that it is too risky for you personally to go into Russia. However, if you insist on going yourself, we would advise that Madame Pickford remain here until you return."

Douglas turned to me. "Well, honey, what do you think? Are you afraid?"

"No; I want to go along with you."

I didn't know until we came out of Russia that he and Floyd Gibbons, the war correspondent, had arranged that if we were not out at a certain hour on a certain day, Gibbons was to fly to a small airfield he knew of on the outskirts of Moscow and try to rescue us.

When our train reached the Russian border, everybody but the engineer got off. It gave me the eerie feeling that we were crossing the River Styx or some similar one-way barrier. I don't recall now the exact width of No Man's Land between Poland and Russia at that time, but it must have been between five and

276

ten miles. We arrived at Minsk at eleven o'clock on a starless and moonless night. In a very primitive, dimly lit customs house, which looked more like a cabin in the northernmost wilds of Canada, our luggage was minutely examined.

While the rest of the party was thus occupied, an enormous Cossack, head shaven and wearing a faded blue cotton tunic, beckoned to me and Lo Rie, Douglas' sister-in-law, to follow him. She and I obediently trailed off into the night, I fervently hoping that one of our party was keeping his eyes on us. Only a dim, tiny electric light shone outside the rickety structure. The huge Cossack, who turned out to be the porter assigned to us, pointed his finger and we saw a tremendous private railroad coach, the windows and doors decorated with branches of fir trees as a token of welcome to us. Suddenly Douglas came dashing out of the customs house, one of the few times I ever saw him violently irritated with me.

"Never leave my side again for any reason!" he shouted. "I don't want you to go five feet away from me! Remember where we are!"

The Polish train returned to Warsaw and, our luggage thoroughly examined, we were soon safely aboard the Russian train. Since the gauge of the Russian tracks is much wider than standard, the coaches are broader and roomier. We were all greatly bewildered by the luxury of the private car we were given to ride in—the ornate furniture, the stately sitting room, the elaborately designed stove—till we learned that it had belonged to the Czar and Czarina. Everything was carefully covered with linen, and the deep, tufted maroon leather underneath was well preserved.

At daybreak we were awakened by a knock on the door. A cameraman was waiting for us at one of the small stations. I had no objection to being photographed, till I made a survey of myself in the Czar's mirror; then I almost screamed. It had been a sultry night and, after laying out my underwear and cosmetics on a table, I had foolishly opened the screenless windows. In that early light the first object I saw was a black pillow, which I had supposed to be white when I fell asleep.

"That's strange!" I said to myself, till I drew my finger across the pillowcase, and from the white streak it left I knew it was soot. I swear I could have appeared as Topsy without any further assistance from the make-up kit. The soot was everywhere. Without orange juice or coffee I started to brush the soot out of my eyes and hair—to confront the pitiless eye of a motion-picture camera.

Very few people realize the tremendous amount of preparation that goes into movie photography. Actresses are at the studio at six in the morning to be ready for the camera at nine. Their hair is shampooed daily, and coiffed by the finest hairdressers in the country. Tests are made for days and even weeks in advance for different colors of grease, paint, powder, and lipstick, to say nothing of different styles of hairdressing. Not one, but several, make-up specialists are needed to prepare them for the camera.

Yet, here I was, wan and groggy from a sleepless night, no breakfast, my hair stiff with soot, and about to be photographed in a dimly lighted railroad coach. I pleaded to be spared this ordeal, but to no avail. I asked the cameraman not to put the camera too close, but again my plea fell on deaf ears. To keep up my spirits, apparently, he would peep out from behind his camera and say, "Mariuska," pause several seconds, then add, "I lof you." Each time I forced a smile and thanked him profusely.

This went on for a good part of the morning. What he did with those thousands of feet of film is still a mystery to me. . . .

A touching little reception awaited us at one of the small country stations some distance from Moscow. A large group of actors and actresses had sat up the entire night on wooden benches in a third-class railway carriage to greet us. They had brought heaps of flowers along, which were now almost wilted. They were gracious and charming, and a little pathetic, in their threadbare clothes. A few of them managed to convey in English how they had seen all our pictures and how welcome we were in Russia. In the company of these men and women of the Soviet stage and screen we resumed our journey to Moscow. Whenever we came to a station we gave to the women and children who greeted us boxes of candy that had been given to us in Warsaw.

After the way these actors and actresses received us, we were fairly sure of a cordial reception in Moscow, but we were not one whit prepared for the staggering crowds, estimated at one hundred thousand, that met us at the station. Young men and girls had climbed up the poles. Hundreds of people pressed forward toward the train, up the steps, and into the coaches. How to maneuver through this immovable mass became a problem in military strategy. Over Douglas' frantic protests the cameraman and a tall official of OGPU with thick glasses grabbed me and half carried me through the train. Each holding me by an arm, my feet scarcely touching the ground, they descended the steps and rammed a path through the crowd. A little boy recognized me, shouted, "Marooshka!" and started toward me, only to be flung aside in the rush, and sent tumbling into an enormous pile of milk cans. I tried to look back

279

to see what had happened to him, but the crowd had wedged in and closed off my view.

My two escorts now rushed me through the large wooden gate of what looked like a government building of some kind, perhaps a post office. As we entered, two men advanced with drawn guns. The police agent showed his credentials and explained who we were. An automobile was waiting there, loaded with flowers and wild strawberries evidently intended for me. Douglas, who was running like mad only a few feet behind us, reached the gate just as it was slammed shut and locked. Suspecting foul play, he climbed up the gate, leaped blindly through the opening in the top, and came down heavily in the middle of the car right on top of all those flowers and strawberries. He gave one wild look at the red blotches on my white organdy dress, and, almost petrified with fright, cried out:

"Where are you wounded?"

"Only in my feet, where you jumped on them."

"What's all that blood?"

"Oh, Douglas, that's only strawberries!"

"Strawberries!" he shouted. "Where did *they* come from?"

"From a Russian admirer. . . ."

At length we reached the Hotel Metropole, ready to collapse from fatigue, only to learn that four cocktail parties and three dinners awaited us. I had just finished my picture *Sparrows,* and was looking like one myself, having lost considerable weight on a diet of spinach and milk. I'm afraid I stalked through those banquets like an undernourished ghost.

Douglas and I spent one week in Moscow—a week of endless receptions and meetings and gigantic feasts. The motion-picture people were with us at all times, attentive, kind, and voluble. And of course we met the director Eisenstein. Before we set out for Russia, we had both seen his masterpiece, *Potemkin*, at a special showing. I told Eisenstein how my hand had frozen to the umbrella I was holding, and how I had to pry it away with the other hand when the picture was over—which was the literal truth. I was amazed to discover that Eisenstein and the others knew as much as our own people, and perhaps more, of what was going on in Hollywood in the way of production, budgets, stories, casts. Even more amazing was their ability to name the American stars who were on the decline and those who were stepping into their places.

They had a million and one things to say about the movies in general, and I couldn't help thinking how closely bound the artists of the world were, however divided their governments might be.

I am sorry I never got to see the inside of the Kremlin. I almost did, because at the end of our visit Douglas and I were supposed to go there together. But the pace had been too great for me, and I had fainted that morning. I remained in bed resting while Douglas went alone.

When Douglas returned to the Metropole that day, he was appalled at the size of the crowd that still lingered before the hotel. They had been there since we arrived. Some would leave and others would take their places. Now it was larger than ever. People couldn't get in and out of the hotel, and policemen charged the crowd on horseback. The crowd would call out our names and we would wave back to them from our window. In desperation Douglas buttonholed an American correspondent who spoke Russian and brought him down to the second-floor balcony to explain to the crowd that I was ill; that

*Oslo, Norway
1924*

Copenhagen, 192

*Kobe,
Japan
1929*

Berlin
1925

Stockholm,
Sweden
1928

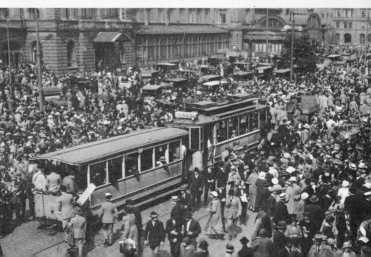

the strain of the visit had been too much for me; that he wanted me to rest because we were leaving Moscow that afternoon, and that at all costs I had to be quiet for the few hours remaining.

When those people heard that—those thousands of Russian men, women, and children massed in the street before the Hotel Metropole—they applauded, but with a moving, unforgettable difference. They applauded without making a sound, bringing their hands almost together, without touching. And when they had done that they quietly went away.

Not all our trips, of course, were as dramatic as this Russian journey. But it seems to me that Douglas and I never returned from any trip without at least one memorable anecdote—sometimes quite an embarrassing one at that!

I am thinking of a visit we paid the Countess di Frasso at the Villa Madama in Rome during the spring of 1933. The Italian Crown Prince, Prince Umberto, was expected one evening and I knew full well that I was supposed to be dressed and downstairs before His Royal Highness and the princely entourage arrived. I was applying cosmetics to the Countess di Frasso when, as luck would have it, an ancient Italian duchess came into the room. Entranced with the work in progress on the Countess's face, she insisted I do as much for her. I allowed myself ten minutes extra to play safe. But turning the Duchess into a Hollywood glamour girl proved to be a bigger job than I had bargained for. The result was that I had to forgo my shower and neglect my own facial requirements. The maid knocked on the door and said:

"Signora, you have but three minutes to get downstairs."

In Paris a few days before I had purchased a lovely piece of lingerie fastened at the waist with a threaded loop and a tiny pearl button. I was hurriedly passing the loop over the button when the maid returned to announce that His Royal Highness had just arrived. Without waiting for my handkerchief or powder case or elevator I flung myself down the great marble stairs, skidded across the sleekly polished marble floors of two enormous rooms, and slid through the majestic archway, where an equally majestic footman announced: *"La Signorina Maria Pickford."*

At that exact moment I felt a slow, creeping touch of descending silk, and I thought, "No, it can't be! It mustn't be, merciful heaven!" Suddenly I stiffened in horror and couldn't move another step. My pearl-buttoned lingerie had fallen and settled around my ankles. Conversation stopped, and for a few agonizing moments a dead silence reigned. If I had had any sense I would have stepped delicately out of the garment and allowed the footman to gather it up for me. Instead I glared at him as if he were responsible for the unfastened button, reached down and picked up the unmentionables, tucked them under my left arm, and proceeded with all the dignity I could muster toward the hostess, who was standing beside the prince. With a deep curtsy I said:

"Good evening, Your Royal Highness."

With that the tension snapped and the whole room burst into a thunder of laughter.

I am reminded of another encounter with royalty when I was again late. During the summer of 1926 Douglas and I were invited to meet the King and Queen of Spain at the American Embassy in Madrid. My maid was ill that day and I had to unpack my clothes and fish out the accessories from a mass of handbags and trunks. Douglas was all nerves waiting for me to leave. In the car, on our way, I realized I had already made my first *faux pas* by forgetting my white kid gloves. When we got to the Embassy, we were told that Their Majesties had already arrived. It didn't help much to learn that three other Americans were late too, having arrived just one minute before Douglas and me.

From the entrance hall I could see the enormous reception room. Seated at one end was the Queen, dressed in pale pink satin heavily embroidered with brilliants and pearls, a diamond necklace, bracelets, and a magnificent tiara. My eyes roved from her to the glittering array of Spanish nobility, resplendent with decorations. Then from the dazzling crystal chandeliers my gaze fell to the highly polished floor, and it was then that I suddenly realized I had neglected something else: to scrape the soles of my brand-new slippers. I now ran the risk of having my feet slide from under me on this slippery floor. And at that moment I realized, too, that I had forgotten to blot the lipstick on my mouth, and here I was supposed, like everyone else, to kiss the Queen's white-gloved hand. I made a silent resolve to remember, at all costs, not to touch the Queen's glove with my lips.

"Now, Mary, my girl," I said to myself, "be calm and take hold of yourself. This is only a motion picture and they are all extras—the King and the Queen included. Hold your head up and walk slowly.

The lorgnettes were now well focused on the two late Americans as Douglas and I proceeded to the presence of the King and Queen. Douglas later told me what was on his mind as we crossed the room together. He was wearing a French decoration, the medal of "L'Education Publique," which he had received while we were in Paris. The closer we got to the royal pair the larger and larger the decoration grew in Douglas' mind, until it was finally preceding him. By the time he was face to face with the King, Douglas was certain he would hear something like this:

"The world, Fairbanks, owes everything to the artist."

And he, Douglas, would in turn say something very simple and very brief, something in the tone of the Gettysburg Address. At length we were presented. The Queen was most gracious. She inquired about her cousins Lord and Lady Mountbatten and asked me if I had seen their new baby Pamela. I assured her that Pamela was one of the most beautiful infants I had ever seen, and that "Dickie and Edwina" were in the best of health. Douglas had meanwhile started a conversation with the King which went as follows:

"Tell me, Fairbanks, what has become of that jovial comedian Fatty Arbuckle?"

Arbuckle had just gone through a scandalous experience that resulted in his forced retirement.

"It is most unfortunate, sir," Douglas replied, "but Arbuckle has been in a great deal of trouble."

"Yes, yes," said the King, "I know all about it. It's really too bad. But that's the sort of thing that could happen to any one of us."

"Her Majesty and I miss seeing his pictures at the palace," the King went on. "We are great admirers of his."

"May I tell Arbuckle that, sir?" said Douglas. "It would mean everything to him."

"Yes, please do," said the King. "Tell him that we miss him and hope he will soon be back on the screen."

Later, while we were standing together on the balcony, the King asked me:

"Do you think that our young ladies are quite as beautiful as those of Hollywood?"

I assured him they were; that, in fact, the lovely girls of Hollywood came from all parts of the world, including Spain, and were not American in any narrow or exclusive sense of the word.

"Come to Madrid to make a picture, both of you," urged the King. "I will put every facility at your command, and I will even appear in the film myself."

I was quite proud of my behavior that day. Though I was late, at least I managed not to smudge the Queen's glove and, what's more, I preserved my balance on that polished floor. As for "L'Education Publique," a slight shock awaited poor Douglas some time later in Aix les Bains. We were both looking into the window of a parfumerie when the shopkeeper rushed out with an enormous atomizer and proceeded to spray us with a perfume he had himself created. Through the haze of perfume Douglas saw that the enterprising little merchant was wearing "L'Education Publique." That was the first time it dawned on him that the decoration wasn't quite in the same class as the Croix de Guerre.

No matter how entertaining and exciting our travels may sound, they were also filled with hardships—for me, at any rate.

Douglas never suspected the effort I made to conceal my distaste and discomfort from him. For one thing there was the

288

question of food. I have always been a poor eater, whereas Douglas could eat almost anything with relish. He loved exotic dishes like the Arab Kushkush. If you've ever had so much as a whiff of that delicacy, you will understand my revulsion; it smells like nothing in the world but a dissipated, ancient billy goat. Douglas not only ate choice delicacies of all the races of man, he went into raptures over their exquisite qualities— things like Chinese bird's-nest soup or hundred-year-old eggs, shark fins pickled, and chickens with their legs, claws, and heads thoughtfully left on. I don't dare mention the other ingredients of that festive fare. My reader is probably already on my side, so I'll desist.

Douglas, born traveler and *bon vivant*, could mold himself into any and all conditions, which I greatly admired in him. But I must admit that I almost exploded at times, particularly when hunger gnawed at my innards. Amid these redolent banquets I lived largely on tea and stale crackers that often gave off a reminiscent smell of cockroaches. Suffice it to say that I used to arrive home from these expeditions in such a willowy state that a strong wind would have carried me from Los Angeles over the bay of San Francisco.

Douglas, I might add here, was the sort of raconteur who would never spoil a story for the lack of a few facts. It was in Hong Kong that I discovered this creative side of his. Newspapermen were thronging about us, and before we knew it Douglas and I were separated, each surrounded by an equal number of reporters and photographers. I soon began to notice that my crowd was gradually thinning out. At length I was left with only two reporters, my crowd having left me to go over

to Douglas. From where I stood I could sense the profound absorption of the reinforced Fairbanks group. I couldn't see Douglas, but I began to hear his voice, and this is what he was saying:

"Just then the camel turned and bit Mary and was about to trample her to death when I rushed over and rescued her."

The camel had sneezed on me; that was true. But that was the full extent of bodily injury I had sustained in that hair-raising episode. My two faithful reporters also caught Douglas' words.

"Where did he bite you, Miss Pickford?" they asked excitedly.

And I had to think quickly.

"On my arm."

"Could we see the bite?"

"Well, there's no point, really, because it's all healed up."

Alone in the stateroom, I asked my darling Baron Munchausen for an explanation of the fabricated camel story.

"It went great, didn't it?" was his exuberant comment.

That settled it.

"Wait till we get to Shanghai," I said. "The things I'm going to tell the press. Before I get through, you won't have one reporter listening to you!" And he didn't!

Douglas and I after a day's work
in "The Black Pirate" and "Sparrows" 1926

In "Sparrows" 1926

20

I sometimes wonder whether I had the right to cut off my hair. Were the choice ever given to me again, I am positive I would not do it.

Shall I ever forget that day at the hairdresser's on Fifty-seventh Street and Fifth Avenue in New York? I had left Douglas at the Sherry-Netherland, a very incredulous Douglas, I must say, when I announced where I was going and why. And here was the coiffeur, a pathetic picture of stifled rebellion and indecision, fondling this avalanche of hair that fell way past my waist.

"Are you sure that you are not going to regret this step, Miss Pickford?" he asked.

I replied, "I'm quite sure. I have thought it over again and again. My curls have become a stumbling block to the future of my career."

"All right; here goes!"

As he gripped the shears I had the feeling he needed aromatic spirits of ammonia more than I did. I closed my eyes when he applied the scissors. Except for the time I wore bangs as a very small child, *it was the first time scissors had touched my head.* I realized the hairdresser was trying to spare my feelings, and no doubt his, by not cutting through my curls. Instead he feathered most of them, with the result that only six of them remained intact. The other twelve curls he "feathered," that is, he put the scissors right through them. Those six curls he let fall on my aproned lap; the rest of the hair was on the floor. I must confess I had a frightening, all-gone feeling as I watched the pile growing on the floor. I stared at the unfamiliar head in the mirror, tried to cheer up the remorseful hairdresser, stuffed the six curls in my bag, and returned to the Sherry-Netherland.

When I removed my hat and showed Douglas my shorn head, he turned pale, took one step back, and fell into a chair, moaning, "Oh, no, no, no!" And great tears came into his eyes.

"But I told you I was going to do it. . . ."

"I know, honey, but I didn't think you meant it. I never dreamt you'd do it."

I must have looked very crestfallen over his reaction, for he immediately changed his tune.

"Whatever makes you happy, dear. After all, they were your curls, and you've done what you thought best."

Neither of us said anything when I took the six surviving curls out of my bag and placed them gently side by side. Two of these curls are now in the Museum of San Diego; two in the Los Angeles Museum; and two at Pickfair.

I had suspected, and probably secretly wished, that Douglas would react the way he did. What I wasn't at all prepared for was the avalanche of criticism that overwhelmed me. You would have thought I had murdered someone, and perhaps I had, but only to give her successor a chance to live. It was a very sad business indeed to be made to feel that my success depended solely, or at least in large part, on a head of hair.

I naturally missed the curls after they were gone. I had always taken care of my own hair; washed it and curled the ringlets over my fingers. But I thought that getting rid of them would free me, and I suppose in a way it did. I began to feel a change, a sense of ease and liberation I hadn't known before. It was my final revolt against the type of role I had been playing. There was no retracing my steps now. I made *Coquette*, my first talking picture, and had the great satisfaction of winning the Academy Award. For that my curls seemed at the time a very small price to pay.

Whether it was because of my new sense of independence I don't know, but I had a very serious clash during the filming of *Coquette* with my most devoted cameraman. He had been with me since we had made *Daddy Long Legs* ten or twelve years before. No cameraman was ever so solicitous of the face he was photographing as he was of mine. There were times when I felt he was its true owner, and I only the wearer. A highly sensitive artist and conscientious craftsman, he was loyal to a fault.

It was in the middle of a crying scene in *Coquette* that I realized my cameraman and I had to part company.

My face was magnified many times as the tears slowly formed in my eyes and I gradually worked up to a hysterical outburst. I know I wasn't a very pretty sight, but weeping never is, and I was thinking only of my grief at that moment, knowing that that was the only way I could make others feel

it with me. In the midst of this intense mood the camera suddenly stopped and I heard my cameraman murmur something. I fairly trembled from the abrupt snapping off of the mood.

"What's wrong?" I asked. "Did you run out of film?"

"No, Miss Pickford; a shadow fell across your face that I didn't like."

I regret to say I lost my temper.

"If I appear as sincere as I feel, no one will ever notice that shadow."

"Let's try it again, Miss Pickford," he said, completely unimpressed.

"But I'm afraid I cannot get the mood back."

Nor could I. There was gloom around the set because everybody else knew I was right. For hours we tried to achieve the same pitch of grief, but failed. The particular mood was shattered and gone. Shadow or no shadow, he should not have stopped his camera. That would at least have given us a chance to examine the shot in our dailies on the studio screen. I made up my mind that it was time our paths should part. I was determined to give the performance of my career, and to give it my own way.

The ending of this sad story is happy, however. My cameraman secured another contract and we remained good friends. I went forth to win an Oscar for *Coquette*. That was in 1929.

Recalling *Coquette* and the Oscar brings to mind a visit I once paid George Bernard Shaw. I had always been eager to meet the patriarchal G.B.S., and was doubly intrigued when I was told he

As Norma Besant, with Louise Beaver,
"Coquette," my first talkie, 1929

had said, in one of his tirades against motion pictures:

"Why should I pay to see a man kiss Mary Pickford, when I can do it so much better myself?"

I regret to disappoint my readers, but that little bit of masculine braggadocio was never put to the test. Indeed, our encounter was very tranquil and prim, the most dangerous subject being tea. As was my wont at such crucial meetings, I arrived late and dreaded the thought of what lay in store for me.

"I was praying that I would die, Mr. Shaw," I said by way of presentation. And that was true.

"But why?"

"Well, as you see, I'm late, I'm ashamed to say I lost the way, and I was afraid of the consequences."

Shaw laughed. "My dear," he said, "I have a confession to make. I'm not quite that formidable. But don't get it about that I am easygoing. I have to keep up the illusion of being a very nasty old man. If I didn't, people of all sorts would besiege me uninterruptedly. Besides, I deliberately chose this house so that it could not be easily found "

The tea appeared.

"Sir," I said, "would you like me to pour the tea?"

"By all means."

"How do you take yours?"

"I don't drink tea, thank you. I'm much too stimulated as it is."

Standing on the mantelpiece was Mr. Shaw's Oscar for *Pygmalion;* beside it a priceless old Chelsea figure of Shakespeare, and I thought how oddly and interestingly the soft tones of this antique porcelain contrasted with the gleaming surface of its streamlined Hollywood companion.

298

21

From the day I learned the truth about Mother's condition, I spent three long years in a hell that only a demon could conceive. For we were both playing a game, she pretending that she didn't know and I concealing my terror from her under a mask of unclouded cheerfulness. When we lived together, I did all my crying in the bathroom, with a bath towel over my face and the faucets running full force to muffle the sound of my sobs. Then I would put iced cloths on my eyes to remove the redness and swelling. Alone, I would have black spells of remorse. I remembered that she was doing something for me when it began; that it was while she was searching for black material for Little Annie's mourning dress that the trunk lid fell on her breast.

And it had been so like Mother not to say a word about the accident till long after it had happened. Indeed, it was on the boat coming back from Europe four months later that she mentioned it for the first time. Something had developed there that worried her; but she said she would not submit to an operation. I pleaded with her to do whatever the specialists suggested; that if they thought an operation necessary she should have it done. But she recalled to me the case of a girl who had worked with her in the Cauncey Olcott company years before. She had undergone a similar operation.

"Mary," she said, "I've had three major operations in my life and I just can't face a fourth—not the kind that poor Josie had."

So we consulted other doctors and tried other treatments that proved much more painful and completely ineffectual. Neither of us ever discussed it in terms of anything incurable; indeed, I didn't realize it was hopeless for some time, and neither did she. At last, when the bitter certainty dawned on me, I feigned greater confidence than ever in her recovery. Just when Mother knew I can't say exactly, but I don't believe she suspected that the end would come as quickly as it did.

I was going through her closet one day and I remarked that I thought it was time to throw away some of the old things she kept there and get herself new ones.

"No, Mary," she said. "I'm thinner now and when I'm stronger, I'm going to have a dressmaker alter them. Believe me, darling, I'll get plenty of wear out of them yet."

So I put them back in the closet.

In the fall of 1927 I gave up my work completely and moved out to Mother's beach house. Douglas went with me. There I remained for eighteen weeks, every day of it, from early morning till late at night, in her company. During that time we read the Bible a great deal. I remember Mother would begin her mornings by figuring out what good deed she would do for the day. This generally meant a sizable check to people less fortunate than we were. Sometimes it was just a loving letter or telephone call to someone who needed comfort or encouragement.

Next to the saddest day of my life was the day Mother asked me to release her.

"Don't ask me to live any longer, Mary," she pleaded. "Let me go, darling. I know and you know that life is eternal. I can't stand it any more and death will be an act of mercy. But I can't go unless you promise you won't grieve and cry over me."

I was too stunned to say anything. It had never once crossed my mind that Mother might want to give up the fight. I choked back my tears. . . .

"Please assure me, darling. . . ."

"I promise, Mother. I promise I won't cry. I know you'll be waiting for me on the other side. Yes, if that's the way you want it, I release you, Mama."

"I couldn't be happy even in heaven," she said, "if I knew you were grieving. Remember, too, Mary, that you will be the head of the family now. You must be brave for their sake."

And she asked me to make one more promise.

"You must never blame yourself for anything, darling. You must never think that you ever displeased or upset me. You are the best daughter any mother ever had. I know how cruel and unjust you can be to yourself. You must promise never to condemn yourself for any imaginary wrong."

Again I gave her my word, and fought back the tears.

"If you think it over, Mary, and the situation were reversed, and you were going before me, you know you would want me to do all the things that I want you to do."

A great calm had come over Mother's face.

"This is the very last time we will speak of it. Let's think of more cheerful matters now."

I don't recall what it was she then told me, but I know it was an amusing story. I was shocked that she could tell me anything funny at such a moment, and yet we both laughed. Neither of us cried that day, certainly not in each other's presence.

It was perhaps two days later that Mother became delirious. Just before she lapsed into unconsciousness, she said to me:

"Mary, put your hand in God's and go with Him, and then you'll be working for the good and not the bad."

While she lay in a coma, I thought of Mother and the marked change that had come over her in the last weeks of her life. She had become a very beautiful woman in a dainty and fragile way. The skin had grown clear and smooth and transparent; her eyes had become bluer. Her black hair, with its few hints of gray, looked more lustrous and alive than ever.

Up to the last moment I hoped and prayed that a miracle would happen and Mother would live. So I wasn't fully prepared for the blow when it fell. I was in Mother's town house when I heard the words, the horrible, crushing words, uttered by my cousin Finley Benson, who was soon to follow her.

"She's gone!"

Instantly the words became both a roaring noise and big white visible letters against a pitch-black sky. The letters went on rising till they were like buildings, and then they toppled over and fell all over me. I threw my arms into the air and was going backward through a plate-glass window when Douglas caught me and (I have no memory of this myself) I struck him full in the face with my fists.

The first thing I remember was the grandfather clock chiming twelve o'clock. I could never again bear to look at that clock, a gift of mine to Mother. For perhaps three or four hours nobody could come near me. I was like a wild animal in the jungle. I am ashamed to say that during those hours I even hated God and said so.

Then through the haze I saw the faces of my brother Jack and my sister Lottie—and I began upbraiding them for not being with me at the moment of Mother's dying. I am deeply remorseful and ashamed of what I said in that frenzy of anguish: my poor brother, who was himself to go in five years, and Lottie, who was to follow him three years later. I was completely out of my mind. I have a few fitful snapshots of sanity that come back through that maddening cloud of grief: being amazed, for example, at Douglas' lips being as white as they were.

What finally brought me to my senses was the sight of my young cousin standing against the wall, her hands covering her face, sobbing violently. I suddenly remembered that she was expecting her baby in another month. I went up to her and put my arms around her and said:

"Please, Verna, stop crying and go home. You know my mother wouldn't want you to risk losing your baby."

"I don't care," she said, "I don't want the baby now, because I won't be able to put it in Auntie's arms. She won't be here to see it."

"How do you know she won't?" I asked. "We have to believe, dear, that she will be closer to us all than ever before."

I persuaded her to go down to the beach where she was staying at my mother's summer home, awaiting the arrival of the newcomer that my mother had so longed to hold someday in her arms.

Mother's house was on Canyon Drive in Beverly Hills, on the direct route to Pickfair. From the time they took her away to rest at Forest Lawn I have never passed that house. Indeed, to avoid it, I go several blocks out of my way every day I spend in Beverly Hills. I remember the last morning I saw it—after Mother had left it forever. I walked through the rooms and looked at all the things she had cherished and loved so dearly; the linens and china and rugs and paintings and silver and crystal. I looked at the two foreign cars in the garage. Those things that we had all given her—Lottie, Jack, and I. I realized then as I had never realized before how ephemeral all material things are; and how futile it was to think of finding even the smallest part of my mother among them. I have never valued such things quite the same way since.

Like everybody that has lost a beloved one, I found myself wondering whether there was truth to the stories of communication with the other life. I was tempted to make an effort to contact Mother. But I knew that she would frown upon such a thing. I decided I would not tamper with matters of that kind. Then I told myself one day that a great portion of grief was nothing but self-pity. I consoled myself with the thought that nothing could hurt my mother again. Nor could anything ever again hurt me as deeply.

It wasn't long after her passing that I began meeting Mother in my dreams. The very first time she was back in her bedroom.

"Oh, Mama," I cried, "I'm so glad to see you. I pray every night that I will go over to your side."

I saw her hold her left hand in front of her face.

304

"Don't," she said, "that's dangerous."

"Will I be with you when I pass over?"

"I can't tell you now, darling. That depends upon what you do with the rest of your life."

To this day I still see Mother in my dreams as she was during those months at the beach house when we played that tragic game of make-believe—smiling and brave, dainty and fragile like a piece of exquisite china. It gives me infinite peace to know that so long as I can dream I shall have my Mother with me.

22

As I look back over the years of my marriage to
Douglas, I now realize that he loved me more than
I loved him—that is, up to the time he realized youth was slipping from him. At that point a strange fever and restlessness
settled upon him, and possibly a growing loss of confidence. I
am convinced it was the need to prove something to himself,
rather than to anyone else, that made him subsequently act the
way he did.

Douglas had always faced a situation the only way he knew
how, by running away from it. That, I think, was where I served
him best. I always preferred to look an issue squarely in the
face, and he counted on that. I often had the thankless duty of
being his "hatchet man." In the enthusiasm of the moment
he would invite someone to come to stay with us for the summer at Pickfair, or promise someone a long-term contract,
only to regret his folly the next morning.

"Hipper, will you fix it?" he would plead. With the exception of one guest who came for the week end and stayed thirteen months I usually managed.

The irony of it was, of course, that it always left the bewildered persons liking Douglas and disliking me. They were all convinced that I was the wall between them and him.

I have already mentioned Douglas' excessive jealousy. In the early years of our marriage I adjusted myself to this fairly well, but it later became a great trial to me. Douglas was even jealous of my mother, I'm afraid, and she of him, which made it a perfect torture for me, loving them both as I did. However, Mother controlled herself, while Douglas wasn't always able to. I have never known a man to read as much as he did into a simple look of masculine approval.

Knowing how hopeless this malady of his was, I did my utmost to keep him from suffering. For more than ten years we rarely went to a restaurant or a night club. I had no companionship of people my own age. They were generally older men, older in fact, than Douglas himself, who came to spend week ends with us at Pickfair. One day Rudolph Valentino made an unexpected appearance on the Pickfair lawn, which, in the warm months, was our outdoor living room. I never saw Douglas act so fast, and with such painful rudeness, as he did in showing Valentino that he wasn't welcome. I didn't even go to downtown Beverly Hills without first telling him where I was going and promising to call from there or having him call me. Since it was all as complicated as that, I seldom went anywhere. At the same time I never asked where Douglas himself had been or where he planned to go. In the beginning I had unshaken faith in him. What I knew later was my own business; something I never discussed with anybody and, if you will

Douglas, Zorro, and I

forgive me something I don't propose to discuss now with my reader. I first began to sense the change in Douglas as far back as 1925, not toward me, but in a general restlessness and nervous impatience. There were spells when nothing satisfied him—his house, his work, his friends. Several times I had to refuse to go to Europe with him. I found I just couldn't keep up the pace with a man whose very being had become motion, no matter how purposeless. The male secretary who accompanied him on those frantic excursions told me that Douglas had reached the point where he couldn't stay more than a night in any one place. When they arrived in a town, the first

thing the secretary did was to buy reservations on trains and planes in all four directions. He could never be sure which one Douglas would decide on after dinner. And he only unpacked what Douglas needed for the night—toothbrush, pajamas, and slippers.

Yet it wasn't until early in 1929, while we were making *The Taming of the Shrew* together, that I saw a completely new Douglas, a Douglas who no longer cared apparently about me or my feelings.

I was talked into doing *The Taming of the Shrew* against my better judgment. I have no qualms about admitting that Katharine was one of my worst performances. I was jumpy and nervous from morning to night while we made the film. The director said to my dramatic coach, Constance Collier, one day, "We don't want any of this heavy stage drama; we want the old Pickford tricks."

I'm sorry I wasn't told this before I decided to make the film. I would have fought it out bitterly. Now that the years have intervened I can see clearly what effect the "Pickford tricks" had on the characterization. Instead of being a forceful tiger-cat, I was a spitting little kitten. And the strange new Douglas acting opposite me was being another Petruchio in real life, but without the humor or the tongue-in-cheek playfulness of the man who broke Katharine's shrewish spirit. Besides co-starring in this film, we co-produced and co-financed it. The usual call at the studio was for "nine o'clock make-up." But Douglas somehow managed to stretch out the daily ritual of his sun bath and calisthenics so that I would be waiting on the set for him till nearly noon. This delay, incidentally, cost us both about thirty dollars a minute.

ouglas and I in "The Taming of the Shrew" 1929

When Douglas finally showed up, he wouldn't know his lines. They had to be chalked on enormous blackboards, and I had to move my head so he could read them. That meant taking a scene over and over again. With dozens of eyes focused on us every minute of the day I couldn't afford to let my real feelings be seen.

The strain and tension of those months was a tragic change from the atmosphere of friendly teamwork that had prevailed in the Pickford-Fairbanks Studio for so many years. Everywhere in Hollywood our studio had come to be regarded as the happiest "lot" of all. And I always felt that the greatest compliment was the love given to Douglas and me by our fellow workers. We were always "Mary" and "Doug" to them.

The set was tense with unspoken thoughts throughout the filming of *The Taming of the Shrew*. On one occasion I wasn't at all satisfied with the way I had done a scene.

"Would you mind retaking it, Douglas?" I asked.

"I certainly would mind," he retorted.

The making of that film was my finish. My confidence was completely shattered, and I was never again at ease before the camera or microphone. All the assurance of *Coquette* was gone.

After *The Taming of the Shrew* I worked on *Secrets*, only to burn the negative and write off a $300,000 loss. Another misadventure followed, called *Kiki*, before I returned to *Secrets*, and made what I consider a creditable picture. Unfortunately *Secrets* opened in twenty-five key cities on the day that President Roosevelt declared the bank holiday. Very few people were

With Reginald Denny in "Kiki" 193

spending money on entertainment in the weeks that followed, and while the film was well received, it was a financial disaster.

I shudder even now to remember the tragic and dismal happenings that crowded with such overwhelming suddenness into those few years. The break with Douglas . . . the costly and disheartening moving-picture failures that followed *Coquette* . . . a major operation, and, most shattering of all, the death within a few years of each other, of my beloved mother, my brother Jack, my sister Lottie, and my Aunt Lizzie.

Before I deal with that last, dismal phase of my life with Douglas Fairbanks, there are a few things I must say about Hollywood marriages. It has long been my opinion that, if our Hollywood people were allowed to work out their own problems, a much smaller percentage of their marriages would end in the divorce courts.

I sometimes wonder whether, in the still, sleepless hours of the night, the consciences of these professional gossips do not stalk them. I myself believe in a final reckoning, when we shall be held accountable for our misdeeds. Do they? If so, they have cause to worry over many scoops that brought them a day's dubious laurels and perhaps destroyed someone's peace forever.

I have always thought it amazing that, under the trying circumstances of the industry, so many marriages do survive. I wonder what would happen to doctors, dentists, factory workers, and bankers if they found themselves exposed to the romantic conditions and temptations of the people of the screen

As Mary Carlton in "Secrets," my last film, 193

314

and stage? To the actress the director shouts out, "When you kiss him, mean it!" To the actor: "Put your arms around her and hold her close, as if you really loved her." Sometimes these scenes are repeated many times. Often they are between extremely vital and good-looking people, only rarely married to one another. The marvel is that happy and lasting marriages do exist among them. And there are a great many in Hollywood who go regularly and quietly to their own church or synagogue, who cherish a home and wife and children, who prefer their private lives to be kept out of the news.

When I joined Douglas in Europe in February after the completion of my movie *Secrets*, I learned that he was infatuated with another woman. Not wanting to make an issue of it, I said nothing to him of my discovery. I had to return to California in May. Douglas followed me two weeks later. In the meantime London was abuzz with rumors and counterrumors which had, of course, reached Hollywood. When, early in June, Douglas asked my permission to go back to London, ostensibly to take part in a golf tournament, I had no alternative but to face the issue. He denied his involvement vehemently. I accompanied him to New York and saw him aboard the *Queen Mary* England-bound. He was still denying any entanglement, but less vehemently, and before sailing he asked me what I intended doing—would I wait for him until he came back? I replied that I would do nothing and that, while he was hurting me cruelly, he was like a man with a high temperature and even if he struck me in his delirium I would not blame him, knowing he was not responsible.

With Leslie Howard in "Secrets"

I must admit that the fault was partly mine. I was trusting and confiding when I should have been cautious and tight-lipped. I opened a chamber of my heart that I was determined to keep sealed from the world, and I had to pay for it. You see, I had received a cablegram from Douglas that had stung me painfully. In blunt language it said that he was planning to remain in England; that he was no longer interested in Pickfair; that I could remain there by myself, if I wished. I then did a foolish, but I suppose a very human and womanly, thing. I showed the cablegram to a lifelong friend of mine. The following day I lunched with her, never dreaming she would invite a newspaper columnist along. Without any beating about the bush the columnist, whom I had known for many years asked:

"What about this other woman, Mary?"

I immediately shrank into my shell and said, "I know nothing about that." I did know, as everyone else knew, that Douglas had been seen visiting "The other woman" in the hospital. And he had been photographed going down a fire escape to avoid the British press.

My friend tore into me.

"Mary, don't be a fool! You've got to protect yourself."

"Please, I don't want to talk about it."

"I think you ought to show that cable to her, Mary," my friend persisted.

"But I don't want the world prying into this thing. It concerns only me—and Douglas."

"He doesn't seem to think so. . . ."

During all the long, torturing months of uncertainty I had had no one to turn to. There had been only Douglas' silence

318

and now this shockingly abrupt cablegram. I longed for sympathetic understanding.

"I'll show it," I said, "but I don't want any notoriety. Have I your word?"

They assured me I had. When the columnist had read the cablegram, I opened my heart to both of them. I spoke as I might be speaking to two friends who were trying to help. I did everything to hold back my tears. I told them I wasn't planning to take any action; that I was sure Douglas would eventually snap out of it; I was certain it was only a momentary thing.

"I've got to be patient with him," I said. "There's nothing I want to say for the present except that I love him. I could no more hurt Douglas than I could have hurt my brother Jack."

I counted so trustingly on the columnist's discretion to protect us both against any sensation; to treat the matter gently, without needless emphasis; to quote what could do no harm, and above all to treat the more intimate details as the confidence of a woman in sorrow who needed a friend and not a public advocate.

I learned speedily of my folly. I had at that time a press representative by the name of Mark Larkin, who watched over my name and career with the ceaseless vigilance and devotion of a fanatic. My meeting with the columnist had taken place on Saturday. Sunday morning, as I came out of church, Mark was waiting on the steps for me, beside himself with emotion. Before I knew what was happening, he grabbed my arm and whisked me into my automobile shouting to the chauffeur:

"Ride down the side streets, George! We might be followed."

From the tone of his voice you would have thought all the

police forces of the world were on our trail. Before I could say a word, Mark was bellowing at me:

"Why did you do this to me? Why didn't you tell me?"

"Mark, in heaven's name, what have I done?"

"Look at this paper!"

I felt the headlines like a blow in the face. I was speechless and sick as I read on. Everything I wanted omitted was there. I was made to sound direct and accusing, when I had wanted to be patient and understanding. Where there had been only heartbreak and hope, a full-size scandal now stared me in the face.

"It's too dreadful for words, Mark," I said. "What am I to do?"

All that day reporters swarmed around both gates at Pickfair. Mark and I worked out a simple statement for the papers in which I made clear that a divorce between Douglas and me was unthinkable; that we still loved each other; but that we might consider a legal separation.

If that was Black Sunday for me, the following Tuesday was blacker still. I was scheduled to be hostess for the Bendix Air Meet at the Los Angeles airport. Knowing that the gossip about Douglas and me had reached everyone by now, I was tempted to notify the committee that I would be unable to attend. General "Hap" Arnold had arranged for me to board a bomber at another airfield, to be escorted by six fighting scout planes, three on each side to the Meet. I knew I could not back out at this late hour.

When I descended from the plane at the Air Meet and heard my name called over the loud-speaker, the thought of those 100,000 pairs of eyes upon me was almost more torment than I could bear. It was like some horrible nightmare in which you

320

suddenly find yourself stark-naked among fully clothed people. The expression on my face in the photographs taken that day told more than words my complete misery and embarrassment. At one point in the ceremonies fifty stalwart fliers stood at attention, with General Arnold at their head. I went down the line grasping their hands. And the friendly and protective look I saw in their eyes was touching compensation and lent me courage for the torture I was going through.

One of the great penalties those of us who live our lives in full view of the public must pay is the loss of that most cherished birthright of man's privacy. Receiving so much from the public, we sacrifice our right to this privilege accorded to others. But we are as human as the next fellow. Sorrow, embarrassment, and humiliation are our heritage too. So we cannot be blamed, in time of crisis, for expecting the refuge of a little privacy. There are many other things I could say about Douglas and me; and there are many who have been waiting for those things to be said. I have preferred to keep them to myself. I have never discussed them with anyone; nor shall I, ever. Suffice it to say that I loved Douglas and was proud to be his wife.

When I first realized what was happening, I asked myself only one question: whom did I love—Douglas or myself? I decided that whatever he felt would make him happy was the thing I wanted for him. There was no ill-will on my part. I believed I understood what was happening. A kind of panic had laid hold of him. There was no faith, no philosophy to help him conquer the situation. Once I had made my decision it was easier for me. I berated myself for thinking that life would now be empty without Douglas. I knew I was being ungrateful to all the creative men and women of the past who at great personal sacrifice, some even of their lives, had contributed toward the blessings of civilization in which I shared so abundantly. I remember how in the middle of a sleepless night the thought came to me that one single spoonful of the front lawn of Pickfair would invite the interest and study of a lifetime. I had never forgotten a documentary film showing a drop of stagnant water under a microscope. What a world of bustling, pulsating activity in that pin point of life!

I came to realize more and more that, exciting as much of my life with Douglas had been, I had been starving certain aspects of my personality. I began to spend wonderful hours in my library. I had always wanted to study diction, but had never found the time for it. I took singing lessons to deepen my voice. I returned to my French lessons. I even wrote a book, *Why Not Try God*, that seemed to bring spiritual solace to many readers. I tried to let no memory of bitterness or recrimination enter my mind. I did twenty-six weekly broadcasts. I even began a long and gratifying round of personal appearances in the picture houses: seven days a week, often five and six times a day—Chicago, Detroit, New York, Boston.

It was in Boston that Douglas called me from London.

"Mary," he said in a faint voice which I barely recognized, "I've been named as co-respondent in a divorce proceeding."

That was the most bitter medicine of all for Douglas, because he loathed scandal. What could I say to him except that I was sorry? I sincerely was.

"What do you intend doing?" he asked.

"Nothing, Douglas."

"I'm so grateful, Mary—the way you've stood by and put up with it all."

That was in January 1934. It wasn't until one year later, on January 10, 1935, that I received my first divorce papers in Los Angeles.

And now followed one of the strangest and most heartbreaking aspects of the whole affair. Douglas changed his mind. He came back to California to try to prevent the divorce. I remember how shocked I was at his appearance; there was still the old vitality and physical glow, but something was gone. It was as though his spirit had fled. In the past I could always sense what Douglas was thinking and feeling. I could even read his face. Now there was nothing to read; only a blank page, and my heart wept for him . . . but my mind was made up. When Douglas saw I was adamant, he went back to England, but returned again eleven months later to try to persuade me not to accept the final divorce papers.

Between his first and second trip home I had a call from Douglas' first wife, Beth Sully, who was, and still is, happily married to Jack Whiting. She asked me to come to her hotel, where she said we would be safer from prying eyes than in mine. Beth could not have been more sincere and affectionate when I arrived. She asked me to listen to a cablegram, some two hundred words long, from Douglas in England. In it he begged her to intercede with me to change my mind; to tell me it had all been a stupid mistake which he regretted deeply; that he still loved me, and would I see him if he came to New York. . . .

"Won't you reconsider taking him back, Mary?" said Beth when she finished reading the cablegram to me.

"Beth, what I knew personally about Douglas was one thing; but when the whole world was brought in on it, that was something else. I no longer have the right to take him back."

"Before you refuse, let me say this. I know and the whole world knows that you are the great love of Douglas' life. Douglas was more like a brother to me than a husband."

I thanked her for the warmth and generosity of her advice. To Beth, as to many other people all over the world, the ending of what had been Hollywood's most idealized romance was an inexplicable tragedy. How much more so was the divorce itself! I recall vividly the grief-stricken look on the face of Judge Lindsay, a frequent visitor at Pickfair, who was now presiding over its darkest chapter.

Six questions were asked of me, to all of which I answered a simple "Yes." The key word was that high-sounding platitude, incompatibility. At Judge Lindsay's request the photographers waited patiently until the trial was over, and the newspapermen did everything possible to spare my feelings. No doubt they all realized they were present at a death.

On January 10, 1936, I received my final papers, and on March 7 Douglas remarried.

Up to this point I have not said much about "the other woman" in my story. I suppose I should be grateful to her, and to Douglas, because unwittingly they opened the path to what was to be a happiness I had always craved, happiness in a tranquil setting of family and motherhood.

At the time, however, there were many bitter pills to swallow. One I remember most clearly is the painful way in which I met Douglas' new wife. Some time after our divorce a famous actress of former years announced that she was leaving Hollywood for good. Along with many others I was invited to the farewell cocktail party at her home. I had no sooner entered the house that afternoon when someone grasped my arm and whispered alarmingly:

"They're here, Mary—the two of them!"

I said nothing.

"Did you know they were coming?" I was asked.

"No."

My gracious hostess had not had the courtesy to inquire whether I would accept her invitation under those circumstances.

Douglas and his new wife were in the other room. In the next ten minutes three women came up and spoke about it to me. Seated before me was Norma Talmadge, who had never been a close friend, but whose love went out to me that day.

"All my life, Mary," she said, "I've wanted to look in my close-ups as you look today." That was her way of bolstering my courage.

The atmosphere in that room could have been cut with a butter knife. At length I decided things had gone far enough, or perhaps I should say had not gone far enough, and that I should do something about it. They were in the dining room and I in the living room. I rose from the footstool where I was seated, and with everyone's eyes on me, walked toward them. Douglas must have seen me, for he came forward and met me halfway across the room.

"I want you to introduce us," I said.

"No, Mary, I can't. . . ."

That was Douglas, always trying to side-step an issue, utterly incapable of looking an awkward fact squarely in the face. Only a short time before that we had both been at a United Artists meeting. I had started out the front door when he stopped me and said, "Don't go out now, Hipper; you'll run into our current wife."

I had started for the dining room alone, when I was stopped again, this time by my dear friend, Tai Lachman, a lovely Chinese woman married to one of our leading producers and directors.

"You mustn't do this, Mary," she said. "She must come to you."

"What does it matter?" I answered. "We must meet. I am the older and it is my choice to go to her. I think it will be less embarrassing for the two of us."

The meeting was easy and gracious; in fact she even fetched me a sandwich and a cup of tea.

"I hear Pickfair is for sale," she said. "What a shame."

"Pickfair has served its purpose," I said. "Somehow material things do not mean as much to me as they once did."

She was so much taller than I that she partially knelt on a chair to be nearer my height.

I could see that Douglas was frightfully nervous; not so nervous, however, that he did not want to show me he still had a lithe, young figure. He had always had a vain little gesture of putting his hands in his coat pockets and pulling the coat tightly about his small and muscular hips. That day he did it again. I will concede that it might also have been a gesture of extreme embarrassment. I will also concede that, in his handsome navy-blue suit, he was still the athletic Douglas Fairbanks the whole world loved.

I remember how amazed I was at the fact that I was studying and watching myself from a distance. I was completely beyond pain. But I was moved more than I can say by the beautiful revelation that came to me from the words and actions of my fellow guests. Their anxiety over my feelings and their desire to protect me—all of that generosity of soul was suddenly, and starkly, revealed to me. It was as though they had removed the armor in which we moderns hide our real thoughts, and whispered to themselves:

"Oh, why didn't I say this to Mary before!"

That knowledge was a great compensation to me. I was made to feel that afternoon that their happiness could not be complete without mine; that we were all in this sorrowful business of life together, and that it was perhaps a kind of self-protection to reach out in sympathy and understanding to each other.

My sister Lottie

328

23

I shall always be glad that Mother did not witness the two tragedies that struck during those few years —the cruel, untimely death of my brother Jack on January 3, 1933, followed in a few short years by the equally untimely death of my sister Lottie on December 9, 1936. They were blows from which, had she been alive, Mother would never have recovered. They left me with a lasting void in my heart, in my early forties the sole survivor of a fond and vivacious family that had triumphed so long and so bravely over the uncertainties of life.

I should like to say here that I am certain both Lottie and Jack would have had a much better chance of professional success if they had not been burdened by the Pickford name. There has never been any question in my mind that Jack was an infinitely superior actor to me.

He had a stark simplicity and directness unlike anything I have ever seen again on the American screen. There was a great

L*

sense of pathos, too, and a keen, shrewd humor in his acting. Those who saw *The Goose Woman, Brown of Harvard, Seventeen, Huckleberry Finn, The Little Shepherd of Kingdom Come* will know what I mean. I am positive that he would have gone farther, much farther, as plain Jack Smith.

Of the two stories Jack's is perhaps the more heartbreaking. Many harsh things were once said and written about my brother. The fact is that he suffered a devastating loss as a young man. I am convinced it was the memory cf Olive Thomas, the only woman he deeply loved, that pursued Jack to the end.

Jack was only nineteen and Olive twenty or twenty-one when they were married. I regret to say that none of us approved of the marriage at the time. Mother thought Jack was too young, and Lottie and I felt that Olive, being in musical comedy, belonged to an alien world. Ollie had had all the rich, eligible young men of the social world at her feet. She had been deluged with proposals from her own world of the theater as well. Which was not at all surprising. The beauty of Olive Thomas is legendary. The girl had the loveliest violet-blue eyes I have ever seen. They were fringed with long dark lashes that seemed darker because of the delicate translucent pallor of her skin. I could understand why Florenz Ziegfeld never forgave Jack for taking her away from the Follies. She and Jack were madly in love with one another, but I always thought of them as a couple of children playing together. They had a host of friends, most of them babies like themselves. When America entered the war, Jack, who wasn't yet twenty-one, gave up a

Olive Thomas, my brother Jack's wife, in a photograph taken shortly before her death

$2500-a-week movie contract and enlisted. Ollie was terrified he would be sent overseas, but they stationed him in Brooklyn, and the war was over before he finished training. There was no wire-pulling for a place of preference or a commission. Jack simply signed up and became an ordinary sailor.

That was how things were when a middle-aged man whom I shall call Dr. Doe entered the picture. He was a doctor in the Navy's induction offices, a confirmed Lothario, and a man of considerable personal charm, but utterly without scruples. Knowing that Jack had many interesting contacts, besides having access to Mother's car and apartment, he proceeded to cultivate him. Naturally my brother was flattered by the friendly attention of this older man who held a position of importance in the service. By degrees Dr. Doe worked himself into Jack's confidence, moved into his apartment, and appropriated his limousine. I believe Jack unwittingly served the doctor as a decoy to attract pretty girls. I know that many times, in zero weather, Jack rode outside with the chauffeur while the doctor sat with his guests in the warm enclosure behind them.

Dr. Doe, however, finally outsmarted himself. To finance his little frolics, he began to accept money to declare inductees either unfit for service or unqualified for anything but office work on the home front. At length he was court-martialed. . . . Then one day Mother, Ollie, and I were thunder-struck to read in tremendous headlines that Jack was being court-martialed along with Dr. Doe. After a lengthy and grueling trial, Jack was completely exonerated.

If a final vindication were still needed, it came after my brother's death when his body was brought back from Paris to California for burial. The Navy offered a guard of honor. Deeply moved as Lottie and I were, we refused, because we wanted as quiet a funeral as possible. And, then, it was too late to erase the great hurt to our hearts, to say nothing of the poor bewildered young heart of a boy who had suffered a cruel and shocking tragedy, and passed on.

The disaster which blighted my poor brother's life still remains to be told. That was the terrible, ironic, and needless death in Paris of his bride of a few years.

I cannot blame the majority of people who know the case only from the lurid newspaper accounts of the time for believing that Olive Thomas committed suicide. Yet I am ready to take an oath that Ollie's death was an accident. Jack told me so and Jack would not have lied to me. Moreover, what he said was fully corroborated by several details of the tragedy itself.

Ollie and Jack embarked on their ill-fated journey to Europe in August 1920. With them were several friends of their age and temperament, among them Bobby Harron, himself destined for a tragic end. Jack told me what follows so often that I can visualize every step of the way.

The night of Ollie's death in Paris she and Jack had been doing the night spots. At one o'clock Jack insisted on taking Ollie back to their hotel, since they were leaving at seven that morning by plane for London. They were already undressed when a crowd of friends trooped in, scolding them for breaking up the party and ordering them back into their clothes to continue making the rounds until dawn. Jack said he was too tired. The crowd finally left. Jack went to bed and Ollie started to write a letter to her mother, outlining their future plans. The unfinished letter was still on the desk after she was taken to the hospital. Jack awakened with the light in his eyes, surprised to see Ollie still up.

"Please come to bed, darling," he said; "it's so late, and I can't sleep with that light on."

Ollie answered petulantly. "You don't care that I can't sleep, do you? I've got an awful headache."

Ollie turned out the lights and went to the window overlooking the street.

"Why don't you take an aspirin?" Jack said, and went back to sleep. Again he was awakened, this time by a crash and a scream. Ollie was standing in the darkened bathroom. Jack rushed to her side.

"Quick, Jack," she said, "turn the light on and see if the bottle with the bichloride of mercury tablets is in the cabinet?"

Jack looked and said, "No, Ollie; only the aspirin bottle is here."

Ollie gave another scream.

"Then I've taken poison!"

Ollie had put the mercury tablets somewhere else, but the maid had evidently placed the bottles, which were of the same size, side by side on the shelf of the medicine cabinet. Jack tried to wash out Ollie's stomach by giving her twelve to fifteen glasses of tepid water. Then he dashed downstairs to secure melted butter and milk. But everything was tightly locked, kitchens and iceboxes, and no one was around but the night watchman. After a frantic search Jack obtained the milk and butter. In the meantime he tried to get the American hospital on the telephone. An ambulance arrived, but only after much precious time had been lost.

Ollie lived for one week, and that one week, according to

the doctors, she owed to Jack's quick thinking in giving her the warm water, milk, and melted butter. But it was a week of agony for the poor darling. When someone who was Catholic entered her room at the hospital, Ollie would look up with those pained velvet-blue eyes of hers and say:

"Please pray to God to leave me with my baby husband!"

She fought a hopeless battle, dying, finally, in my brother's arms. As if that were not torture enough, Jack had to wait an entire week while the French authorities made a painstaking investigation of the case. Finally they were satisfied that it was an accident and not suicide.

Jack crossed the ocean with Ollie's body. It wasn't until several years later that he confessed to Mother how one night during the voyage back he put on his trousers and jacket over his pajamas, went up on deck, and was climbing over the rail when something inside him said:

"You can't do this to your mother and sisters. It would be a cowardly act. You must live and face the future."

I was waiting at Mother's house in Hollywood when the car arrived and Jack stepped out. He walked ahead of the rest of the party, dressed in deep mourning, his shoulders drooping, his head bowed. I remember I had a clutching feeling at my heart that it would not be long, a few months, perhaps a few years, before Johnny would follow Olive. Although Jack married twice again no one could ever take the place of his darling.

His next wife, Marilyn Miller had the attractiveness and sparkle of youth, but I always thought he looked upon her as his child rather than his wife.

Perhaps if they had had a baby themselves it might have been different. Jack always wanted children, but for Marilyn a

career came first. She was probably the most ambitious human being I have ever met. I remember her blinding migraine attacks; one in particular which she had during a singing lesson. The pain of it must have been inhuman, yet she gave not the slightest sign of discomfort. It was astounding to see that kind of determination in such a round, soft, pink and white body. A baby, needless, to say, had no place in a life of such unsparing professional drive. Inevitably the two of them were divorced.

Jack married once again—another Ziegfield girl, who told me she had seen the back of my brother's head in a restaurant and said to a friend:

"That's the handsomest back of a head I've ever seen and I'm going to marry that man."

It was a turbulent union, also ending in a divorce; which was especially sad because Jack needed a loving wife more desperately than ever during those final months of illness and torment.

The last time I saw my brother was at Pickfair. He looked dreadfully ill and emaciated, and his clothes hung on him as if he were a clothes hanger. I remember the wave of faintness that came over me. We had started down the stairs to the automobile entrance.

"Don't come down with me, Mary dear," he said. "I can go alone."

I stood at the top of the staircase and the inner voice said to me. "That's the last time you'll see Jack."

Jack died in Paris. The place he chose for his last days was one from which he could see the window of the hospital room where his beloved young wife Ollie had died thirteen years before him.

Jack and his second wife, Marilyn Miller

It was only four years after my brother Jack's death and eight years after my mother's that I lost my beloved sister Lottie. . . . Poor Chuckie, she was never the same after Jack's going. They were so very close in temperament and even in looks. It was as though with my brother's passing the better part of her had died too. A serious heart condition developed and Lottie was in and out of hospitals after that.

I remember vividly the first image that passed through my mind the night I heard that she had died. I saw us as children out chasing sleds in Toronto, hooking our own to the big horse-drawn sleighs. Suddenly Lottie was catapulted from her tiny sled into a bank of snow. I rushed to her side in terror, certain that she was dangerously hurt, and pulled her out of the snow. That lovely pink face of hers and generous mouth were covered with snow; even the long, dark eyelashes were white with it. I saw her brightly colored, tasseled stocking cap, and I became dizzy with the wave of love that swept over me. I gave my unspoken thanks to God that Lottie was safe. I thought to myself, "This is my very own little sister." That was my first realization of what sister love was, and the picture, in all its myriad hues and emotions, is indelibly stamped on my mind and heart.

The last time I saw Lottie she was taking a piano lesson from a young colored girl. Lottie had gone into ecstasies about the girl's voice, wagering a dollar that I couldn't hear her sing the hymn "Oh, Jesus, When I'm Sad and Lonely" without crying. I accepted the bet. Once the girl began to sing, Chuckie never let her eyes waver from my face. The girl sang in a high, true voice, faultlessly accompanying herself at the piano. As the song progressed, I could feel a very small humming-bird's egg forming in my throat; and slowly grow to chicken's egg size. By the time

338

it reached the proportions of an ostrich egg, I decided it was better to pay the dollar. The three of us then talked about two little books I had written. This in turn led to quotations from the Bible and in kissing Chuckie good-by, I quoted from Jesus:

"'Where two or three are gathered together in My name, there am I in the midst of them.'"

And I added, "I'm sure He's been here with the three of us today."

That was the very last time I saw my sister.

The doctors told me that Chuckie was stricken so suddenly that she probably died standing up. I was greatly consoled by a story a young seamstress told me about Lottie's last days. This girl, Annette, whom Lottie had befriended in her typically generous way and had set up in the dressmaking business, said that she visited my sister the day of her death; Lottie had just awakened from a nap.

"I had the most wonderful dream," she told the seamstress. "I dreamed I was in a very large church filled with flowers, little children, and beautiful music. I went out into the garden and saw Jesus standing there. He took my hand, and together we walked through the garden. He even talked to me but I can't remember what He said."

It was then and will always be a consolation to me to know that almost the last person my sister was with, if only in a dream, was this gentle Friend whom she worshiped so simply and deeply.

*With Buddy Rogers in "My Best Girl,"
my last silent film, 1927*

24

When I was a girl of fourteen, playing in New
Haven with Mr. Belasco's company, I went out
one day and sat in the park by myself. As I watched all the
Yale students strolling by I had the feeling that if I looked
closely enough I would see my future husband, or someone
very much like him. Always in my heart I carried a picture of
what he would be like. I knew everything about him, his complexion, his eyes, his voice. Douglas Fairbanks was many things,
but he wasn't the original of the picture I had hung up in my
heart, nor was Owen Moore. Actually I didn't meet the man of
my girlhood vision until the day a friend of mine introduced me
to Charles Edward Rogers, better known as "Buddy" Rogers.
Fantastic as it was, I immediately thought to myself: "What a
pity I didn't meet him in New Haven!"

The first thing that struck me was his blue-black hair, so like
my mother's, that lay in thick waves on his beautifully shaped
head. I remember how becomingly it matched his long navy-

blue coat, for Buddy was a University of Kansas dandy. The next thing I noticed was his dark brown eyes. There are no eyes quite like Buddy's, the eyes that look out upon the world completely without guile. I knew at once that this was a man who would put the idea out of his mind if ever he thought the world was otherwise than good. In the eighteen years we have been married I have not seen the slightest hint of suspicion or mistrust of anyone.

I, who grew up in Toronto, New York, and Los Angeles, have never known the warmth and friendliness of a small town. Buddy came from Olathe, Kansas, and I think its townspeople must go out of their way to live up to its name, which in Indian, I understand, means "beautiful." The people all know one another, and Buddy told me that his father, Probate Judge B. H. Rogers, knew the names of every single family in Johnson County. The Rogers are the kind of family that not only I but all America can be well proud of.

I met Buddy in 1927. I had no more idea that he would one day become my husband than I had of marrying the King of Siam. Actually it was not until ten years after the first meeting that I became Mrs. Charles Edward "Buddy" Rogers.

The attentions of such an attractive young man were naturally a wonderful help during those years of loneliness that followed the final break with Douglas. Although I saw very little of Buddy since he was traveling with his orchestra, I will say this: more than anything or anyone else, he gave me back my desire to live. A rather sad but delightful compliment was

With Lucien Littlefield and Buddy Roger
in "My Best Girl

paid to me by Buddy while I was still married to Douglas. When people asked him if he ever intended to marry, he replied in his direct manner:

"No, the woman I love is already married."

That the reference was to me was generally known to newspaper people. Out of respect to a marriage everyone idealized, no one ever so much as hinted at it in print.

At first I put the thought of another marriage far from me. When Buddy proposed, I rejected him, naming one reason after another. Finally I was confronted by a new and very determined Buddy. This was several months after the divorce in 1936. I was in California and he in New York. I received the following ultimatum from him:

"Mary, the time has come for you to make up your mind whether you want to marry me or not. It is foolish to go on this way. You know exactly how I feel. It has never been a secret to you or to anyone else that I have loved you from the beginning, long before you knew I existed. If you do not want to marry me, then in all fairness to us both you must let me know. It is entirely up to you now. I shall never bring it up again."

I immediately telephoned him in New York.

"Buddy," I said, "you're absolutely justified. I've got to make up my mind."

"Will you marry me?"

"Yes. I would be happy to be your wife."

"Thank you, honey!"

When Buddy joined me in Hollywood, he put the question to me once more and of course my answer was again yes. That night he called his father in Olathe, Kansas. We hadn't intended

344

to give the news to the press yet, but the beloved Judge, who had married several thousand people in his life, was so excited that he released the story to the Kansas City *Star* a few hours later. Mrs. Rogers then came to California and we gave a dinner party for our closest friends and family at which the formal announcement was made. That was November 19, 1936.

The following June, Buddy and I were married under a large sycamore tree at the home of Hope and Buddy Lighton, who had introduced us ten years before. Only our most intimate friends and family were there. Those spreading branches above us were sacred as church spires to me. I prayed fervently, as I do now, to make Buddy happy, for he deserves it. I don't believe to this day he has stopped telling everyone I am the only woman he ever loved.

Except for Chuckie's daughter, Gwynne, I had lost my entire family. When I married Buddy his family now took the place of my own loved ones, and Buddy's mother helped me to bear those dark moments when against every resolution I found myself brooding over the loss of my mother.

Once before I married Buddy, Mrs. Rogers and I were on a train together when a telegram reached us, addressed to "To my two sweethearts."

"How marvelous it must be to have such a fine son," I said to Mrs. Rogers.

And she, a conservative woman of very few words, turned to me and said:

"Mary, I owe you so much."

"I don't think I understand."

"You see, Mary, knowing how you loved your mother, no one could be near you and not love his own mother more."

Judge Rogers, myself, Mrs. Rogers, and Buddy

As for Buddy himself, I confess I don't always understand him. At times I find him aloof, self-contained, undemonstrative; a complete introvert. I am just the contrary, a complete extrovert. This presents difficulties, but it is also a stimulating element in a marriage. We have spent weeks on end alone together and gone on long trips here and overseas, and never once longed for the company of others. No woman ever cherished anything as I did my new-found happiness with Buddy. In the end I believe that Douglas himself, jealous and possessive as he had been even during our years of separation, was happy for me. We were all in London for a company meeting. Buddy accompanied me to the Korda Studio, and there Douglas gave him a thorough inspection. After the conference, while I was waiting for Buddy to pick me up in the car, Douglas took me aside.

Buddy and I—June 26, 1937

"Well, you're a good picker, Mary; he certainly is a handsome guy."

"And he's even nicer than he's handsome," I replied.

It was during that visit to London that a weird coincidence occurred. One day a little Irish maid read my tea leaves. I'm not superstitious, not really, though many people think I am incurably so. What she said interested and puzzled me.

"I see someone stretched out lifeless; he is close to you and he is not close to you. He is either dying or dead, but I don't see you crying."

The next morning the London newspapers called to say that Owen Moore had been found dead on the kitchen floor of his house in Beverly Hills. There had been a cerebral hemorrhage and Owen had been dead in the kitchen for two days. The date was June 12, 1939. Now this may be a pattern and it may not; it may be superstition or mere coincidence: Douglas died exactly six months later, December 12—on Owen's birthday.

The night Douglas passed on Buddy and I were at the Drake Hotel in Chicago. It was the third year of our marriage. Buddy had put in a hard day with his orchestra and we had been asleep for two hours. At four o'clock the telephone rang, and Buddy answered it.

"Mary, it's Gwynne," he said.

I took the phone.

"Don't say it, Gwynne! He's gone, isn't he?"

"Who told you?"

"No one, but I know."

"Yes, Auntie, Uncle Douglas is dead."

And she started to cry.

It was then that Buddy showed his usual tact. He asked if instead of going back to sleep I wouldn't prefer putting on a warm dressing gown and staying up with him.

"I'll send the bellboy out for some warm milk or tea. How about it, honey?"

And we stayed up, the two of us, drinking milk and tea, shivering in the cold, and talking; talking about everything under the sun but Douglas. Out of respect for Buddy I would not weep. In fact I did not cry until I was New York-bound on the Twentieth Century the following evening. Then I let go.

Unlike Douglas, who so often evaded reality, Buddy is a solid individual who can be counted upon in emergencies. He is utterly unspoiled, and although his good looks might belie the fact, he is essentially a man's man.

One of Buddy's secret horrors is to be suspected of trying to promote himself or get special attention.

During World War II after Buddy joined the Navy I had a long talk with the wife of one of his fellow officers. She told me how the boys had made plans to give Buddy the "works" when he arrived. "A movie actor!" "A band leader!" "A so-called handsome guy!" They had it all worked out how Buddy was to be put in his place. Her husband, while agreeing in substance with the others, thought the thing unfair.

"You've got no right," he said, "to judge a man because of the way he earns his living, or because of his looks. I have as much use for a glamour boy as the rest of you. Why don't we give the guy a chance to prove we're wrong?"

"Mary," this young officer's wife said to me, "my husband would jump overboard for Buddy."

Buddy and I, 1942

There was only one thing lacking to make our marriage complete—children. . . . I had been deprived of motherhood by a surgeon's inefficiency when I was much younger. Under the circumstances I suppose it was just as well. Owen would have resented a child as another intruder demanding attention, and I'm afraid Douglas was not the paternal type.

"Hipper, children often destroy a happy marriage," he would rationalize. "You're all the baby I need or want."

The longing for motherhood was to some extent filled by the little children I played on the screen. Through my professional creations, I became, in a sense, my own baby. And when Lottie's baby, Gwynne was born, that was a blessed day in my life too. Some years after Mother's death Lottie said to me:

"Mary, how does it feel to have been able to give Mama everything her heart desired, and all the fame and honor besides?"

"Chuckie," I replied, "how does it feel to have given her the baby? I'm going to ask you a question, Lottie. Put all the worldly things on one side of the scale and the baby on the other side. Which in your estimation outweighed the other in Mama's heart?"

"The baby, Mary."

There was no question about that. The joy that Gwynne had brought into all our lives could not be measured and we both knew it.

It was my little niece Gwynne, incidentally, who once sized me up to perfection. She was twelve at the time and I overheard her say to my cousin Verna, "Don't go in there now; Auntie is in one of her quiet, dangerous moods." That struck me as so funny and so true that it broke whatever spell she seemed to think was upon me at that moment.

If I had all the children I have wanted to adopt, I would today be the mother of at least twenty. I had maternal designs on every baby that played with me on the screen.

I believe I began my baby hunt the day I married Buddy. I soon realized it was going to be a long and arduous search. I discovered that one agency alone in Los Angeles had a waiting list of 2700 married couples.

The day we met Ronnie, Buddy and I had actually gone to interview a little girl. It is a curious thing about the psychol-

351

ogy of adoption—almost the instant your eye rests on a child you know whether or not you want him or her for the rest of your life. The little girl we went to see was eight years of age. Much as I love children, I did not feel that immediate surge of affection for her.

While I was making up my mind that this was not the girl for me, Buddy had wandered into the courtyard, where some children were playing. As he watched them his eyes returned again and again to one particular boy. Buddy noticed how considerate he was of the other children. They were playing ball, and the little fellow kept insisting that everybody be given a chance to throw it. Buddy asked an attendant if the boy were available for adoption. When he heard that he was, he said he wanted to introduce him to me. So they washed the boy's face, combed his hair, and hustled him into a fresh little suit.

The door of the courtyard opened, and in walked Buddy with one of the handsomest boys I have ever seen in my life. When Buddy introduced him, the little chap gave me a smart salute and a firm handshake. In the meantime the little girl had left the room, and the three of us were alone. The boy climbed up on Buddy's lap in a very possessive manner. Buddy now began a rapid-fire exchange of double-talk with me. What did I think of the proposition? Fine, I said. Remember, it's a long term contract, he warned.

"I'm willing to sign it right now," I said. "What do you say?"

"Absolutely!"

So the bargain was sealed. The following Sunday we called for him and he spent the day with us. I never saw a child eat as much and as often as he did that day. When it was time to take

352

Roxanne (four) and Ronald (ten)

him back, he wept so bitterly that it all but broke my heart. I couldn't close my eyes that night. A week later he was permitted to come to stay with us. Ronnie was six years of age when he became ours.

After Ronnie came Roxanne, ten months later. I suppose everybody knows that in most of these homes they never let you go near the young babies. Mrs. Rogers accompanied me and we looked at dozens of little babies through a glass window.

"What do you think of this little one, Miss Pickford?" the head nurse asked me.

I looked and couldn't take my eyes away.

She was five months old, with the blackest hair imaginable. First she looked at Mrs. Rogers, studied her face and gave a toothless grin, her head wobbling from side to side. Then she gazed at me with two big dark eyes, and the toothless grin spread over her sweet little face.

Well, I went home and I couldn't see anything but that baby's face. More than I ever wanted anything in my life, I wanted that baby, and wanted her at once. There were formalities, of course, and, oh, how nervous they made me. I made countless telephone calls to the home.

"Well," they would hedge, "we think her back is rather weak."

"The more reason why you should give her to me. I'll get the finest care for her."

"We'll have to take her I.Q.," they said.

And I replied, "If you take mine, I'm certain you won't give her to me, because I know I'll never pass."

Finally they asked me to come down to the office. With me were Mrs. Rogers, Ronnie, my secretary Mrs. Lewis, and the

354

faithful Yvonne, my French maid, who later became the children's nurse and governess. They remained behind in the car while I went into the office. There I was given a little ticket.

"What's this for?" I asked.

"It's for your baby."

For a moment I was stunned by the sound of those two words. What a thrill that was: "Your baby."

Then I dashed down the steps and shouted into that carful of people, "Look, I can have the baby!"

"But, Miss Pickford, you can't do that!" said Yvonne. "We have no bottle; we have no clothes, and there's no place for her to sleep."

"I'll borrow everything! And she'll sleep with me!"

I was so excited I never once thought of calling up Buddy at the air base to tell him he was about to become a father. I am ashamed to say I had absolutely nothing on my mind but that bundle of warm life awaiting me.

It seemed a century before the nurse finally appeared. The next thing I knew the baby was in my arms. It took Ronnie and the three women to hold me up as I climbed cautiously into the car. I passed the baby to Yvonne and took the wheel. All the way home I was figuring on putting my baby in a clothes basket all nicely padded and covered with a pale pink silk bedsheet. I think I went at least twenty-five miles with the brakes on, whizzed through red signals, and arrived at Pickfair in a cloud of fumes and dust.

Her surprised daddy's first comment when he saw her was, "Gosh, she's little; oh, she's awfully little, Mary!"

"She'll overcome that in time," I assured him.

My first problem was where to put her. I turned to my devoted and resourceful housekeeper, Agda Erickson. "We're going to need a clothesbasket, Agda."

Without further instructions she disappeared and in a few moments was back with a perfectly beautiful bassinet.

"Agda," I exclaimed, scarcely believing my eyes, "where did you get that?"

"Oh," she said, "it once belonged to a former employee who lived on the grounds. I found it in the storage room."

Of course I was up all night trying to keep the covers on Roxanne. I didn't have the sense to fasten her in with safety pins. The following morning I went to her daddy with my first problem.

"Buddy, the baby is scratching her face with her fingernails. They're too long."

"Why don't you cut them, honey?"

"I'd be frightened of hurting her."

"I'm not," said Commander Rogers. "Get me a pair of cuticle scissors."

I'm ashamed to say I couldn't bear watching him, so while he knelt down beside her, I slipped out of the room. I could hear him talking to her.

"You're a nice little thing."

To make a long story short, she wrapped up her father in a package, and she's never let him go. When Roxanne first said, "Daddy boy dear," Buddy's face looked as though it had been carved out of a block of ice cream and put into a hot oven.

There is at least one awkward moment that comes up in every case of adoption. Mrs. Rogers came from Kansas for the birth of my niece Gwynne's first child. This was about six months after Ronnie's adoption. I called for her at the Pasadena Station and took Ronnie along with me. On the return trip Mrs. Rogers was seated in the back and Ronnie beside me. He was so small that I am certain Mrs. Rogers completely forgot he was there.

"You must be terribly happy, Mary," she said, "at the prospect of a Pickford baby."

I made some sort of evasive answer.

"Think of it," she went on, "a baby of your own flesh and blood."

I could feel Ronnie's body stiffen beside me. I had to think fast.

"Well," I said. "You never know how they will turn out and of course you can't make your own selection the way you can the other kind."

Mrs. Rogers caught my eye in the mirror, and understood. There was a moment of silence, and then Ronnie spoke up.

"You were very lucky, Mother."

"Yes, I know, but you tell me why, darling?"

"Well, you could see exactly what I looked like, and that was very lucky for you."

My friends often ask us about Ronnie and Roxanne. One of the most frequent questions is whether we knew the children's background. Yes, as a matter of fact, we did—not only about their parents but about their grandparents too. Roxanne's father died on Guadalcanal, and her mother, who never recovered from the blow, died when Roxanne was five months old; that is, one month before she came to Buddy and me. Ronnie's parents were English, Irish, Scottish, and French, which is exactly my mixture. Roxanne is Irish, German, and Dutch. Except for the Dutch strain that is parallel to Buddy's background.

Our children, I should add, have grown to look very much like
each other. Buddy and I consider ourselves lucky indeed to
have been thus blessed not once, but twice.

25

Each of us has at least one moment in his life that stands out with a burning sense of shame and self-guilt, a moment during which we committed a grave, though perhaps unintended, offense against a fellow human being. Some have the power to efface the pain of that moment from their minds; others find solace in appeasing their consciences by one means or another; still others have known how to distill a deeper understanding of themselves and others from their honest remorse.

I believe one of the most thoughtless things I ever said was an intolerant remark I made one night in Beverly Hills to two Jewish friends of mine. One of them was Carmel Myers, an actress, beautiful, talented, and of rare intelligence and character. She and I have the same birthday, and it is a source of great pride to me that she always calls me her sister. The episode occurred at the time Hitler had begun his savage campaign against German Jews. Both she and her husband were quite properly denouncing this inhumanity, when, unthinking fool that I was, I tried to explain it as a situation that the Jews had partly brought on themselves. I said something about how wealthy Jews had bought up German properties at bargain prices after World War I, how I had heard that some American Jews had formed syndicates to exploit the depression in Germany. Even before Carmel spoke I knew in my heart that I was describing only a very small minority of that historic race—a minority that one can find among any people.

"Mary," Carmel said simply, "I will make only one comment to that. You must never forget that before we are Jewish or gentile, we are all human beings."

I am sure Carmel Myers has forgiven me that lapse from grace, inexcusable as it was. That she will ever forget it I doubt. Such jolts to the spirit, particularly when administered by a trusted and intimate friend, are not easily put aside. Carmel, however, never knew this, but she will know it now: because of that intolerant outburst I was so ashamed of myself that I went home that night and got down on my knees. I asked God to forgive me and show me the right path to help these persecuted people. I repeated that prayer every night for several weeks. I made up my mind that I would answer the very first appeal from the Jewish people with my whole being; that I would somehow make retribution for a baseless slander of a defenseless minority that was now being crucified as no other people had been in all history.

"Mary," I said to myself when I rose from my knees, "you're not a poor Christian; you'ı ɲo Christian at all. You have still to prove to yourself that you really believe in Jesus and the things He taught."

As if in answer to my prayers, my opportunity finally came. I received a letter from Ida Mayer Cummings, sister of Louis B. Mayer, inviting me to speak at a donors' luncheon on behalf of a Jewish home for the aged. Knowing that the subject was very close to my heart, she asked me to speak about mothers. An association began with that luncheon that has blossomed into greater beauty than I ever thought possible. I had been taught as a child that love begets love; but I found it now a plainly demonstrable fact. By serving my fellow men and women, with no desire for gratitude and completely eliminating myself from the picture, I was serving God. And that love came back to me a thousand-fold.

The donors' luncheon now became an annual observance in my life. Ten or twelve such meetings have been held on the grounds of Pickfair, and often as many as twenty-five hundred women were present. I don't think I was the very first gentile to join the organization, but I was among the first. At present it is Jewish-gentile in membership. Nor does the Junior Auxiliary confine itself to Jewish welfare alone. During the war I saw with my own eyes the splendid teamwork of these tireless and dedicated women. They gave their time and energy to blood banks and canteens, entertained the boys in their homes, drove them around in their cars; cared for the wounded—all of it nonsectarian. Every civic and national appeal found them willing and ready soldiers of the one Father.

Then Mrs. Cummings and the ladies of the committee applied themselves to the urgent need for additional beds for the aged. Many of these Orthodox Jewish men and women were billeted in a home across the traffic-ridden Boyle Heights Boulevard, where there were no facilities for kosher food and spiritual services. Now the truly Orthodox Jew would rather starve, according to his understanding of the highest good, than eat food that is forbidden to him by his faith. So these elderly people, many of them halt and partially deaf and blind, would make six trips back and forth across that strip of death when they went to their meals and to "Schul." And of course some of them were injured and killed.

"It's very simple, Ida," I said to Mrs. Cummings. "We'll build a new home for them."

"You really believe we can raise the money?" she asked.

"I know we can."

We started with the plans for twenty beds, added twenty more, then increased it to sixty, and finally we had one hundred beds subscribed for. During the twenty-bed period, Louis B. Mayer, in a flattering tribute to me as a motion-picture pioneer, announced that he would double his donation of rooms if the building were named after me. And that is why the five-story, one-hundred-bed home is now called, "The Mary Pickford Building."

This whole experience has taught me another great truth: that when we desire to aid others, and to aid with love, that very moment, puts us in tune with God and with all good people everywhere.

These are my new "babies"—these old men and women of the Jewish faith. I have never been a *"schiksa"* to them, that is, a gentile woman. When they address me or speak of me, it is always as *"mammale"* and *"mammochka."* On many different occasions they have intoned their prayer, *"Mische berach,"* for me. When I underwent a major operation, many of them were carried and wheeled into their places of worship, remaining at

362

prayer in "Schul" from the moment I was placed on the operating table to the moment I was safely back in my room.

I know now that, despite the ugly things that are still happening in the world, the children of God, those who truly love Him, are growing closer all the time. And whether we are Protestant, Catholic, Mohammedan, Reformed Jew, or Orthodox Jew, wherever the love of God and truth is, there He is too. Nor does He exist only in the temples of wood and stone, for we have been told that each of us is a temple within himself of the living God.

With
Peter Sammartino,
President of Fairleigh
Dickinson College

*President and Mrs. Eisenhower buying
the first Treasury Bond, April 1, 1953*

*Speaker of the House, Joseph Martin,
buying a Treasury Bond*

My birthday in Atlanta, Georgia, 1953.
With Joseph G. Woodruff during Bond tour

26

It requires no great powers of deduction to realize that Pickfair was named from the first syllables of my name and Douglas'. However, it was neither Douglas nor I who named it. That wedding of the names was the inspiration of some unknown newspaperman. I have always thought it far too pompous a name, for one would naturally picture a huge estate, stables and all, instead of a fairly large, comfortable home. I suppose it is with houses as it is with people; they have their personality in the eyes of the people who behold them. The newspapermen got into the habit of referring to "Pickfair" as a "mansion" and a "palace." I think I was beginning to believe it myself, when I was brought to earth by an Englishman who asked me one day:

"Do you still live in that charming little cottage, Miss Pickford?"

Children of both sides of the family have grown up at Pickfair, and they have always brought their friends along with them to play on the grounds.

While Douglas was not paternal in his thirties and forties, his attitude changed decidedly in his fifties. He then reached out to his son. I was grateful for the wisdom that was mine during the early years of our marriage when I encouraged Douglas, Jr., whom we called "Jayar," and the four Fairbanks girls, Douglas' nieces, together with my own niece Gwynne, to swim at our pool throughout the summer. On Fridays we always dined early and watched a movie. Invariably I made myself scarce when Jayar was with his father, because I wanted them to be alone together. In the last few lonely years of Douglas' life he sought his son's companionship and found great comfort and happiness therein. I am proud to say that I still possess the confidence and love of Jayar and his family.

It is a great pity that Douglas did not live long enough to see his three lovable granddaughters. And how proud he would have been of Jayar's courageous war work as a Commander with Louis Mountbatten, for which he earned a special citation from the British Crown.

Life with Buddy and the children is certainly different from the old days with Douglas. The constant round of lavish parties has given way to quieter and more personal entertaining. But Pickfair is still a proud hostess. Proudest perhaps is the memory of entertaining the boys who left our front gates to embark directly for the South Pacific, and to return to us crippled and disfigured. Many of them still swim in the pool and sit under the shade of the wide-branching trees of our lawn—the blind, the lame, the armless, the legless; even the maimed of the First World War.

During the summer of 1949 we had as guests forty blind soldiers of the First World War from the Sawtell Veterans Hos-

Roxie, Buddy, myself, Butch, and Ronnie
—Christmas, 1948

pital. I was told that these men as a group had not been out of
the hospital in thirteen months. The party we had together on
the Pickfair lawn that day has since been an annual rite. As
long as Pickfair belongs to Buddy and me those men will be
with us every summer, and at Christmas, too. I'll never forget the day Dinah Shore came up and sang for them, and how
they sat around on the lawn listening hungrily to the many
songs that went from her heart to theirs. Then they all asked,
"Mary, where is the pool?" And I told them where the pool
was in relation to the house; how many trees there were, where

A U.S.O. party at Pickfair

they were, and how far apart they were from one another. I told them just where the front entrance was and how long and wide the pool was.

One day an officer and an enlisted man came to Pickfair to ask if they could have the grounds for a meeting of an amputee organization that had just been formed. They explained that they hadn't the money to rent an auditorium or assembly room. I told them I would be delighted to have them come with their wives and children.

The day of the meeting arrived, and I am sorry to say my courage failed me. I just dreaded the thought of seeing all those fine boys in and around the pool without their limbs. Coward or not, I decided to stay in my room, at least till the men had done their bathing and put on their clothes. Buddy, who had promised to stay with me a little while, was drawn into the day's

Pickfair

activities earlier than he expected. Having seen some flower petals and bees on the surface of the pool, he went down with the skimmer to clean the pool early that morning. True to form, he had on his old bedroom slippers, worn down to the heel, and a pair of bathing trunks that had been mended, besides which he hadn't shaved. There was Buddy, skimming the top of the pool when a few early birds arrived. So Buddy remained with them all day.

Meanwhile I sat miserably in my room wondering what to do. I had reason to be worried. Some months earlier at a Pickfair party for a group of newly blind soldiers I had lost control of myself. I was able to stand seeing two or three of the boys, but after that my voice broke, and I recall what an effort it took to pull myself together. I knew that the last thing a wounded man wanted or needed was pity; that all he asked was an opportunity to prove his right to a place in the normal life of a community. That experience should have prepared me for my first meeting with my amputee friends, but it didn't. When I finally went downstairs I realized how foolish I had been. I walked over to the pool and was with them as if they had been any other gathering on the Pickfair lawn. In a quick flash I caught the array of artificial legs clothed in socks and shoes, of arms and hands, of babies crawling gaily among them, of happy young mothers chasing after them—and I suddenly realized that everything was perfectly normal. There seemed to be no cause for shock or sorrow. The bright sun shone down on a group of the healthiest and clearest-headed human beings it had ever been my happy lot to behold.

One three-year-old infant picked up his daddy's artificial leg, with sock, garter, and shoe attached, and toddled around the pool, tripping and picking himself up. The laughter that roared from those hundred amputees and their wives is still ringing in my ears.

I controlled myself beautifully that afternoon, but for one lapse. That was when one of the soldiers whose arms were gone above the elbows rebuked his wife for wanting to carry a chair for him.

"Damn it," he shouted, "I'm still a man!"

And, to prove it, he picked up two chairs with his hooks— old American chairs that would have been impossible for me to carry—and, as the tears came to her eyes and mine, marched with determination across the lawn to the porch where the entertainment was to take place.

I was profoundly touched and honored when I was asked to sponsor this group of high-spirited young Americans. I wish I

were big enough, important enough, rich enough, to head every
such organization in this country and every other country in the
world. To have put a few facilities at the disposal of these men
and their families has alone made Pickfair and its hospitable
lawn a place of warm memory and beauty to me.

The main hall at Pickfair

27

One night when I couldn't sleep I whiled away the hours by taking inventory of the various names and nicknames that had been fastened upon me from my earliest childhood. I was appalled at the number that drifted back from the past, and I wondered whether with the going of each name there had also gone the particular identity it fitted.

In the old Biograph days, of course, I was "Goldielocks," "The Girl with the Curls," and "The Biograph Girl." My niece Gwynne often refers to me as "The Bird Woman." To her husband I am "The Mighty Mite." To Jack and Lottie I was "The Big Stick," sometimes affectionately, sometimes not. For a while they switched to "The Policeman," and on those occasions, when they thought I was putting on airs they called me "The Czarina."

While D. W. Griffith always called me "Pickford," Marshall Neilan ("Mickey") always referred to me as "The Tad," a friendly Irish expression. David Belasco called me "Betty."

My scenario writer and lifelong friend, Frances Marion, addresses me as "Squeebie Skunkface of Squatville," if she feels particularly tender, and Errol Flynn calls me "Moo," because, as a child, he had a governness named Mary, which he could only pronounce "Moo." Louella Parsons calls me "Baby Martin" and "Martin Jr." after her late husband, Dr. Harry Martin, who addressed me as his "baby." Marion Davies always introduces me to her friends as "My illegitimate child by Calvin Coolidge," a title she first bestowed upon me when that blameless gentleman was in the White House.

Douglas had a hundred names for me, though the one he used habitually was "Hipper." I'm not at all sure whether that wasn't originally the name of a German battleship. In any case, it also appeared in the English jingle "Eenie, meenie, hipper-de-dick . . ." I don't know where I got "Duber," but that was the name-mate of "Hipper" during our marriage. Douglas also called me "Cute," "Little," and "Critic," though where he got the last one I don't know, because it was lovingly said. When he was slightly annoyed he had two names for me—"Frin" and "Frit." Where they came from only he knew.

There is, of course, one nickname, if I may be so bold as to call it that, which was fastened upon me early in my career, a nickname involving an honor which has always touched me deeply but which I scarcely deserved or accepted.

A prominent Hollywood producer asked me if I would relinquish the title of "America's Sweetheart" for a promising young protégée of his. I answered that the title wasn't mine to give, that, in fact, I had never accepted it, but that such as it was it had been conferred upon me as a gesture of love by an old and beloved friend.

376

The title was the inspiration of "Pop" Grauman, a pioneer movie exhibitor of San Francisco and father of Sid Grauman, perhaps the greatest showman the industry has ever produced. Pop put the title "America's Sweetheart" in electric lights for the first time in 1914, when he was showing my first version of *Tess of the Storm Country* in San Francisco. It was never a publicity "stunt," which makes it, to my way of thinking, all the nicer.

During the war, in 1918, I was marching down Market Street in San Francisco at the head of a Red Cross parade. Hundreds of soldiers and Red Cross workers were marching along together. Flags were flying, bands were blaring, paper coiled through the air; the police were holding back the crowds. Suddenly, through the police lines, I saw a white-haired old gentleman break away from a policeman and, waving frantically, run toward me, shouting:

"Mary, sweetheart!"

The policeman dashed after him. Certain he was a dangerous crank of some kind, he was raising his club, when I ran up to him and cried:

"Don't, officer, this man is my friend!"

The truth is I hadn't the slightest idea who the white-haired gentleman was. I had practically to gallop to regain my position at the head of the parade. The old man was now marching along at my side.

"How's my boy?" he suddenly asked me. "Is he all right?"

"Oh, fine!" I replied without turning my head. I was convinced by then that I had a lunatic on my hands.

"How is Sid's Million Dollar Theatre in Los Angeles doing?" he asked.

It was only then that I realized the gentleman at my side must be darling "Pop" Grauman, whom I had never met—the man who had announced my engagement to the country we both loved and served.

Almost twenty-five years later I was back in Toronto as guest of honor to eight hundred young World War II aviation cadets. Everything was all right till they began singing, "Let Me Call You Sweetheart."

Then I looked out over the hall at the bright, ruddy faces of these young men soon to go overseas, some never to come back, others to wish they hadn't; it was more than I could bear. Despite my firm resolution and the overgenerous mascara on my eyelashes, the tears started rolling down my cheeks. And how the mascara stung my eyes and nose! I can only say, in all humility, that it is good to have lived to know that after so many years off the screen, there were young men, soldiers soon to embark perhaps on their last journey, who could still pay me the sweetest and most gallant compliment of all—to ask to be called their collective sweetheart.

During Red Cross drive in 1918

EPILOGUE

Some years ago I sat for an unusual portrait. The artist was not a painter, but a pianist, his material not paint and brushes, but the black and white keys of a piano. This painter of portraits in sound was the gifted and sightless Alec Templeton.

I thought his impression amusing, but rather puzzling. I could not quite understand an ever-recurring insistent high note. It seems to be restless, questioning, and challenging. I asked Mr. Templeton what that particular note symbolized in his musical conception of me.

"That note, Miss Pickford, is your purposeful attitude towards life and your career," he replied. "It also expresses your readiness and determination to face a situation squarely."

"That is interesting," I said, "but I think there was something more in your mind. . . ."

"That's true," he replied. "That note is the driving force, the high C of your being—the need for action, the refusal to stand still. That suspended high note represents your abhorrence of finality."

Now this may or may not be a true picture. I have known sunshine and shadow. I have opened and closed many chapters. I am today a happy wife and mother. Our home is an invitation to the luxury of prolonged rest and leisure. As long as I live I shall remain profoundly grateful for a past I could never have had without the devotion and loyalty of my family, of unnumbered friends, of movie-going audiences the world over. That is my life up to now, and my book. While I would not have missed that Yesterday I have no desire to go back and live it over. For me now there is only the great Today and the promise of Tomorrow.